JASON
PRIESTLEY

JASON PRIESTLEY

A MEMOIR

with Julie McCarron

HarperOne

An Imprint of HarperCollins*Publishers*

HarperOne

This is a work of nonfiction. The events and experiences detailed herein are all true and have been faithfully rendered as the author has remembered them, to the best of his ability.

HarperCollins books may be purchased for educational, business, or sales promotional use. For information please e-mail the Special Markets Department at SPsales@harper collins.com.

HarperCollins website: http://www.harpercollins.com

HarperCollins®, ▰®, and HarperOne™
are trademarks of HarperCollins Publishers.

FIRST EDITION

Designed by Level C

Library of Congress Cataloging-in-Publication Data is available upon request.

ISBN 978–0–06–224758–2
ISBN 978–0–06–235987–2 (BN)
ISBN 978–0–06–235986–5 (BAM)
ISBN 978–0–06–234529–5 (Intl)
ISBN 978–0–06–235789–2 (CN) For sale in Canada only

14 15 16 17 18   RRD(H)   10 9 8 7 6 5 4 3 2 1

To Naomi, Ava, and Dashiell,
you give me purpose . . .

Preface

My friend the actor John Hurt used to say that people in the public eye have a public life, a private life, and a secret life. I'm not sure that's true for me. Since I was barely out of my teens and began playing Brandon Walsh, wholesome heartthrob of *Beverly Hills 90210*, I've lived a much more public life than I ever wanted. It's hard to keep big secrets in the fishbowl of fame.

I was always ambitious, but the goal was to become a successful working actor. I never imagined the level of fame starring on an iconic show would bring. Writing this book took me back very vividly to that time and place—I remembered all the fun, the camaraderie, the good times and the bad—plenty of it played out in public, much of it misrepresented, and, sure, some of it private . . . until now, anyway.

Still, I've never been one to spend much time looking in the rearview mirror. All my life I've been moving forward as fast as I could, looking for the next thing. So to write this book was not easy or done without plenty of hesitation and false starts.

Twenty years ago I "graduated" from high school on *90210* . . . pretend, of course, but a milestone nevertheless. And ten years ago I literally died and came back to life, slowly, painfully, and with a completely different attitude. I wanted to change my life . . . and I did . . . again. There have been all kinds of major changes—ups, downs, and hurdles—in my life since I arrived in Hollywood as a seventeen-year-old kid, full of boundless energy and a determination to succeed.

I still wake up every morning racing toward my next goal, full of energy, feeling young. Then I see the middle-aged guy in the mirror, the one with a wife and two little kids. The three of them are so all over my business I couldn't have a secret life now if I wanted one! But every once in a while I look back, laugh, and shake my head, remembering. . . .

Rehabilitation Hospital of Indiana 46254

I wake up in a strange room, looking at an unfamiliar ceiling—a not-infrequent occurrence. I feel a little woozy; I'm obviously under the influence of something—again, not exactly an unheard-of state for me. I hear the familiar gentle snore of my French bulldog, Swifty, and turn my head . . . painfully. In the near dark I can make out his familiar boxy form, curled up alongside my girlfriend, Naomi. Hmmm. Seeing them is a welcome surprise. But . . . where are we?

I try to sit up and can't. I realize that I'm wearing a back brace and it's keeping me from moving. I turn my head the other way and see a wheelchair next to my bed, along with an IV stand. A line from the IV bag runs straight into the crook of my elbow.

I struggle to lift my head just an inch or so; then I see my feet, wrapped in fluorescent green casts, resting like two huge misshapen blocks at the end of my bed. It's beginning to sink in. I am in the hospital. I have clearly been in a bad accident. A shock of pure alarm shoots through my body at the thought of being paralyzed. I wiggle my toes with all my might and am vastly relieved when I see them move.

I EVENTUALLY FIGURED out that I have crashed my Infiniti Pro Series car in turn two at the Kentucky Speedway. Speed at impact: 187 mph. I had qualified second for the race that day. The crash happened during warm-up.

I had driven through a patch of Quick Dry, an absorbent material not unlike kitty litter, used to clean up oil and antifreeze on racetracks after accidents, a typical occurrence in racing. That's all it was. An accident.

I had been coming to briefly and fading back out just as suddenly. Each time I gain consciousness I have no memory of waking up before. All I know is that I am now suddenly awake, confused, and in pain.

I find out I was in critical condition in a Trauma ICU in Kentucky before coming here to Indianapolis, Indiana. As I begin the painful physical process of putting my body back together, I also begin the emotional journey of figuring out how I got to this place in my life. You have a lot of time to think lying in a hospital bed twenty-four hours a day.

I got everything in my life through my drive to be successful and my desire to be the best at everything I attempted. I had a fierce competitive spirit that brought me here . . . but this time, I had gone too far.

Vancouver
V6B 3A4

When I was five years old, I told my mother, "I want to be one of those people who live inside the television."

Now, *why* I wanted to live inside the television set in that particular time and place—Canada, the 1970s—I can't imagine. Kids' programs included such gems as *The Beachcombers, The Friendly Giant, Mr. Dress-up,* and *The Littlest Hobo.* We got a couple of big American shows like *Sesame Street* and *The Electric Company,* but for the most part the programming was all ours. It didn't matter; I watched them all and wished I was there. From as far back as I can remember, I had an innate fascination for and desire to be part of that world.

Fifteen years later my childhood wishes would be fulfilled. As the star of one of the most iconic American television shows of the late twentieth century, somebody, somewhere in the world is always watching me, no matter what the day or time. Playing Brandon Walsh on *Beverly Hills 90210* has assured my place in pop culture for all time. I really will live inside the box—forever!

MY PARENTS MET as students at the University of Victoria, where my mother was a star performer in the drama department and my father built sets. He was also an outstanding rugby player, sailor, and all-around athlete. Both were quite artsy and liberal. Mom danced in the

Royal Canadian Ballet before their marriage and continued to work as an actress occasionally after they moved to Vancouver and started a family. My sister, Justine, arrived first. Then I came along sixteen months later.

Mom's agent was a woman named Ramona Beauchamp at the Ramona Beauchamp Agency in Vancouver. Ramona was one of the few prominent show business agents in the area—this was long before my hometown became known as Hollywood North. She signed both my sister and me, and one of her agents, Fiona Jackson, represented us. We were quickly booked for several print ads—not surprisingly, posing as brother and sister.

Probably due to my long straight hair, big blue eyes, and sweet face, I was frequently mistaken for a girl. When strangers would approach my mother to say something complimentary about her "little girls," I would growl, "I'm *not* a girl!" and startle the hell out of them with my surprisingly deep voice. Still, it was the right look for the time: peace and love, hippie hair. I booked quite a few print and catalog jobs, which soon led to every kind of acting gig that was available in the tiny local industry at that time: mostly voice-overs and local television commercials. Justine had no desire to continue after doing a few shoots; I pestered my mother constantly for more work. She was by no means a stage mother; the desire was all mine. From where? Who can say? It was hardwired into me.

One afternoon Mom accompanied me to an audition for a movie at that monument to '70s architecture, the Canadian Broadcast Corporation building in downtown Vancouver. By this time I was an old pro at auditioning. I went in and met the casting person, read my lines, and assured them that I was a strong swimmer (apparently a prerequisite for the part). Fortunately, Dad had had me in the water since before I could walk, and I could not only swim but was also a pretty good little sailor.

Maybe my aquatic skill was the deciding factor in winning the role; maybe it was that I resembled the actress who was to play my mother; maybe they just liked my reading. At the age of six I had already figured out there was a lot of luck and intangibles involved in landing any role at all, even for a tiny ad in the local paper. Many kids couldn't stand the rejection of not landing a part. It only made me more determined. One year earlier, at the age of five, I had begun in earnest to will my dreams to come true; now the power of persistence had landed me my first break.

Vancouver
V6B 0A1

The CBC movie *Stacy* was about a woman with two young boys who suffered from bipolar disorder. In what was one of the dramatic high points of the film, Stacy suffered a breakdown and I, playing her young son, wandered off and drowned in the ocean. There was a long shot of me floating motionless, facedown in the water. As promised, this was no problem as I excelled at the dead man's float.

Coincidentally, a neighbor who lived around the corner, an assistant director who was a friend of my mother's, was working on this movie too. He offered to drive me back and forth to the set. As we turned onto the quiet road where the first day's shooting was to take place, an ambulance went racing past us in the other direction, sirens wailing and lights flashing. I turned to watch it go by and then immediately forgot it in the excitement of reaching the set. The isolated house on the water was a beehive of activity; people in headsets were rushing around; there were huge lights and cords and rigging everywhere.

My neighbor parked his van in a makeshift parking lot where people were busily unloading more vans full of mysterious equipment and smiled at me. "Ready to go, Jason?" he asked, and the two of us began walking. A harried woman with a clipboard came racing up to us and said, panting, "Thank God you're here!" In my six-year-old mind, I thought she was referring to me. Of course, she was talking to my neighbor. "We've got a big problem!"

"What is it?" my neighbor, the second assistant director, asked.

"The lead actress playing Stacy got here an hour ago and said she wanted to explore the house, get a feel for the place. I said fine, so we went inside, and walked around a bit.

"On the second floor, she walked out on the balcony, leaped off, and broke both her legs."

"*What?*" I was immediately forgotten.

"That was our lead! They just took her away in an ambulance!"

"We have no star? What are we going to do?"

"I'm on it . . . I already reached out to the casting director. She called our second choice, who's on her way. She'll be here in about twenty minutes."

"Thank God!" The two assistant directors started walking toward the house, deep in conversation. I was completely enthralled. A crazy lady jumped off a balcony? And broke both her legs? And no one even missed a beat. Production kept moving right along!

Our neighbor remembered me after walking a few yards and called to me. "Come on, Jason. Come with us and we'll get you squared away. It's going to be a couple of hours."

I ran to catch up. I could not have been happier with the way my day was going. Things got even better later on. I was given my own custom-made wet suit to wear under my clothes for my climactic scene. I felt very important and starlike. I had never worn a wet suit before, much less one made to measure.

I floated in the freezing water of the harbor in the middle of a Vancouver winter, a diver hovering just out of the frame for safety. I felt perfectly fine and toasty warm. But as the cameras started to roll and I leaned forward to put my head down for the dead man's float, icy water gushed into my neckline and trickled all the way down to my toes inside my wet suit. Talk about cold. It was bitter! It wasn't hard to remain motionless; my entire body went absolutely numb within seconds as my mind went blank. Fortunately, the director got the shot he needed in just two takes; I was probably only in the water for a couple of minutes and was immediately whisked into a warm towel and rubbed down and blow-dried back into warmth. That part was fun, too.

The showbiz lessons were starting early, and *Stacy* was the perfect example of the first and most important rule for an actor to absorb: Can't get the job done? Next! The show must go on. Also, I could see that "stars" were not necessarily the most mentally stable and together people. Third, being an actor meant there were lots of cool things to do and perks to be won—like my very own wet suit.

I had only one thought as my friend drove me home late that afternoon. *Man, I love this business!*

North Vancouver
"North Van"
V7J 2X9

I wasn't exaggerating when I promised the *Stacy* staff that I was comfortable in the water. A lifelong avid sailor who had grown up spending his free time at the Royal Victoria Yacht Club, my dad transferred his membership to the Royal Vancouver Yacht Club after he married, and he bought a twenty-four-foot sailboat. From the time I could walk, we were out there on weekends working on the boat and sailing and racing.

Boating was always a big part of our family life. Being on the water is something that I absolutely love to this day. Being under sail, no noise from the engine, having the wind move your boat through the water . . . it's intoxicating. Eventually, my parents cobbled together enough money to buy a gorgeous new thirty-three-foot sailboat and we took an idyllic weeklong family vacation. The weather was simply spectacular, and everyone was happy. I recall it as pure joy. My sister and I were in heaven, swimming, fishing, playing in the sparkling water. Everyone was happy. Or so I remember.

Which made it quite a tremendous shock when my parents split up soon afterward. In fact, most of my memories are blank surrounding their actual divorce. There had not been any fighting or yelling or any signs of trouble; they were good at hiding their unhappiness from us. They reassured us both that it was nobody's fault, that they still loved us. They did the best they could, but it was still devastating.

Dad moved to a bachelor apartment in the West End for a while. Mom looked for a full-time job and taught classes at Ramona's agency on weekends. The beautiful new boat was sold. I lay in a sleeping bag on my dad's living room floor on weekends, stunned at the sudden sweeping changes in my life. It was the '70s, and divorce was rampant; families were breaking up everywhere. I was just one more kid among millions with a weekend dad and a broken heart.

Windsor House
"North Van"
V7P 2M3

Windsor House School was exactly what you would imagine a small school run by a hippie in early-1970s Canada to be. Windsor had been founded by an innovative woman named Helen, who taught in her own home; the school eventually expanded into a proper building with a bunch of teachers. But it stayed quite alternative and progressive; all the teachers were hippies as well, many of them musicians. This was right up my progressive mother's alley; Justine and I were both enrolled there from kindergarten on.

What I remember most clearly from those days is sitting in a circle around our teacher, Corky, as he played his acoustic guitar while we kids sang "Up on Cripple Creek," "Kumbaya," and other folk songs. Corky had crocheted a brown vest for himself with a huge lightbulb shooting rays of light in yellow on its front. He wore that vest every single day, rain or shine, hot or cold. Deodorant was not something anyone at that school cared about. That was fine in the winter, but things got mighty fragrant in the spring and fall. Lunch was always raw almonds, millet, greens . . . which funnily enough seems quite trendy and acceptable now. But back in the age of processed foods? It was simply unheard of.

Truly, there was a great deal of sitting in a circle and listening to guitar music, though we must have learned our ABCs and numbers and how to read somewhere along the way. I had a strong pragmatic streak even as a child; I knew this wasn't exactly the way school was meant to be. Still, I went along with the program docilely enough for several years.

During Caveman Week in the fourth grade, we all dressed up in ratty old furs and grunted, using sign language as we pretended to be cavemen in the basement of the school. We were given actual dead fish to use as props as we pretended to catch food by hand like real caveman did. The fish, our food, were then stored on shelves in our "caves." Some of the fish, of course, fell behind the shelves or were discarded someplace else, and as the week wore on they began to rot. The whole place smelled horrible. Beyond awful.

None of my fellow "cavemen" seemed to be bothered. When I tried to talk to them about how we should deal with the rotting fish and resulting smell in our midst, nobody was particularly responsive. That included the teachers. It was at that moment I realized it was definitely time to seek new educational opportunities.

On the way home from school my sister and I talked it over, and that night I spoke to our mother. "Listen, Mom, I can't do this anymore. I need to go to a real school. With classrooms and workbooks and stuff. I'm not learning anything at Windsor House." It was agreed that starting in fifth grade I would attend public school, and Justine would join me there.

It wouldn't be until years later, when I had children of my own, that I would realize I was receiving a great education at Windsor House. I only had the confidence, as a nine-year-old, to question my mother's educational choices for me because of the type of education I was receiving.

Windsor House is still going strong and is a beloved and well-respected school in Vancouver.

On Set
Vancouver
V5X 3X8

Fletcher's Meats was Canada's equivalent to Oscar Mayer—a purveyor of breakfast meats. The company was looking for kids to star in a series of three commercials, and I landed one of the roles. A kid named Bernie Coulson was cast as my brother. We did look somewhat alike; he, too, had blond hair and blue eyes. The two of us hit it off right away. Bernie was fun. He had a mischievous gleam in his eye and was an explosion of energy.

Seven years later we'd be in a crappy 1967 Coupe de Ville on our way to L.A., but for the moment we were ten- and twelve-year-old kids, wearing goofy '70s clothes for "summertime fun" commercials. We all sang a song that went: "I love Fletcher's, it's the most fun you can eat; wieners, bacon and sausages, ham and luncheon meat. You can put it on the bottom, you can put it on the top, you can make it up all fancy, you can feed it to your pop. . . ." There was plenty more, but you get the idea. Dear God. It was all so very . . . 1979.

This series of three commercials played constantly all summer; there was no escaping them if you lived in Canada and turned on your television. They didn't do much for me besides get the crap beaten out of me in the school yard on the first day of fifth grade at my new school.

I wasn't paid a tremendous amount, and in Canada, with its significantly smaller population, residuals were not nearly what they would be for a commercial in the United States. Still, the money I earned on the commercials was enough to buy my heart's desire: a YZ80 two-stroke dirt bike. It was pretty much the perfect vehicle for breaking your arm. I managed not to break any bones, although a couple of my friends did.

While I enjoyed my new bike, Vancouver's nascent film and television business ebbed and flowed; it went into a very quiet period for the next several years as the Fletcher's commercials mercifully faded from the airwaves. I returned to my regularly scheduled childhood.

Vancouver
V5T 1R1

During my high school years (the real ones), I kept myself busy in the theater department.

Delta High School had a beautiful new theater and a genius drama teacher named Ilene Jo Roitman, who also taught the comedian and *MADtv* actor Will Sasso.

The summer in between my junior and senior years I got a call from Fiona who asked, "Hey, what are you doing? Want to work as a stand-in on a film called *Hero in the Family*?" It made for a nice break from painting houses and crewing on boats at the Vancouver Yacht Club. I immediately accepted the job as a stand-in and stunt double for an actor out of New York named Christopher Collet. The film was a Disney Sunday movie of the week, a wacky comedy about an astronaut and a chimpanzee switching brains that also featured a teenaged Annabeth Gish, who later appeared on *The X-Files* and *The West Wing*. I kept my distance from the chimp and soaked up the atmosphere.

An older woman, a British actress named June Whitaker, showed up for a few days to shoot a small role. I could see, just watching the few scenes she appeared in, that she really knew what she was doing. This woman could act, so I started paying attention to her off-camera as well. Before they called action, June stood off by herself making faces and gestures; I couldn't imagine what she was doing, so I approached her one day and asked, "What were you doing just before they shot that scene?"

"Preparing," she said. "Working on my instrument . . ."

I was lost. "What's *that*?"

"I teach acting, you know. Why don't you come to one of my classes and see what it's all about?" she said.

"I will," I promised her.

I had taken lots of acting classes, with several different teachers, but there was something very special about this woman. She was approaching her work differently than I had ever seen before. I soon learned that June had arrived in Vancouver from New York five years earlier and opened an acting school. She was a part of the Neighborhood Playhouse in New York for thirteen years prior to that and introduced a new level of teaching to Vancouver. Over the next five years, June's school would produce countless successful actors from Vancouver: Bernie Coulson, Nicholas Lea, Christianne Hirt, and Martin Cummins, to name a few. Her teachings of the "Method" could be controversial, but also very effective. I met her at just the right time in my life when I was looking for more. I knew I needed to become a better actor. I knew I needed to grow in order to bring more to my work, but I didn't know how. I was passionate about learning all that she had to teach.

As soon as *Hero in the Family* wrapped, Chris Collet got cast in an episode of *The Hitchhiker,* and I moved along with him to serve as his stunt double/stand-in once again. Chris then returned to New York and completely fell off the show business radar. I returned to painting houses for the last couple weeks of the summer to earn money for June's classes and prepared for my senior year of high school.

By that time I was working steadily and traveling to Los Angeles to meet with agents.

I was laser focused on the new life that would be mine in less than one year. Most of my friends were looking forward to enjoying a great senior year and preparing for college. Of course, my training didn't end with June, but the time I spent with June and in June's class changed the way I thought about acting. My path was set. I was a working actor already. I knew then that a move to Los Angeles was in the offing for me. It was just a question of when.

Lower Lonsdale
"North Van"
V7M 3K7

I enrolled in night classes at June's school and was soon completely immersed in her training. I knew very little about Method acting, and even less about improvisation. June's course involved a tremendous amount of improv exercises that threw me at first, but which I soon came to enjoy. We did lots of one-on-one and group improvs; I found them all to be incredibly beneficial. This training forced me to learn to think much more quickly on my feet, as well as how to be more naturally reactive in the moment.

Who should show up in acting class right around the time I joined but my buddy from the infamous Fletcher's Meats commercial, Bernie. Immediately, we were thick as thieves again, playing off each other at improvs, laughing, telling jokes, having a blast. There were other teenagers in our class as well as middle-aged moms, kids, and retirees: a full spectrum of ages. This wide cross section of people made our interactions very dynamic. June made sure everybody was matched with the right partner and groups to get the most out of the experience. She was an inspiring teacher and pushed me hard to excel. Every minute I spent in her class was valuable.

IN THE FALL of my senior year, Fiona called me to alert me of a new
FOX show called *21 Jump Street* that had begun production in Vancouver. I auditioned for one of the first-season shows and was cast in
an episode called "Mean Streets and Pastel Houses." The show was
about the punk rock scene and a group of disaffected middle-class
kids who fall under the spell of an evil but charismatic punk rocker. I
played a kid who called himself Tober—short for October, "the time
of year when everything dies," as one of my lines read.

The company was shooting late at night in a local park. I parked
my motorcycle on the street and walked over to where I saw a few guys
I knew from around the Vancouver acting scene. We were all waiting
to be told what to do when a young guy in a studded black leather
jacket walked right up to me and said, "Hey, how are you doing? I'm
John," and stuck his hand out.

We shook as he asked my name. "Jason, great. The director's on his
way over and we're gonna get this thing going here in a few minutes.
Need some coffee? It's right over there. Sound good?"

It was very cool that the star of the show was so warm and gracious. The way he greeted me that first night of work made quite an
impression. Johnny Depp was a polite, friendly, all-around great guy.
I was a high school kid, feeling a little uneasy my first time on a new
set. Having the star of the show, the guy who was number one on the
call sheet, come right up to me, ask my name, and shake hands set an
example I appreciated and try to emulate to this day.

Shortly, I was sent over to the makeup trailer. I had long hair at
the time—actually, I had a mullet going—so it took a while to slick
it all down and refashion it into a faux Mohawk. This is something
that would never happen today; producers and audiences demand
authenticity. Now an actor would have to shave his head and wear a
real Mohawk for that part. But fortunately, this was the 1980s, and my
beloved mullet was spared.

As I sat in the hair chair being prepped, the trailer door opened and
one of the most stunning girls I had ever seen walked in and plopped
herself down in the makeup chair. She was young, as were all the cast
members in this show about undercover police officers, but clearly a

bit older than I was. Holly Robinson was the only female regular on *21 Jump Street*. I could not take my eyes off her. Our eyes met in the mirror, and I smiled. She smiled back, then quickly looked away.

A production assistant rushed into the trailer and handed Holly some new script pages. "Freddy's done some last-minute rewrites to your scenes," he said, and rushed back out.

"Of course he has," Holly murmured and shook her head, rolling her eyes just a bit, but only kiddingly. Freddy was Fredric Forrest, the actor who played the captain on the show for the first six episodes before being recast with Steven Williams. Apparently, last-minute rewriting took place quite frequently. Holly and I made some small talk about Vancouver and there was an obvious attraction between us. When my complicated hairstyle was done and I was summoned to the set, I made some lame comment about hoping to see her later and exited. *Smooth.*

The crew had the scene all set up and ready to go. I sat in the backseat of a car, taking a last deep breath, when all of a sudden the door popped open and director Jim Whitmore jumped in, shoved me over, and sat down beside me. He looked me straight in the eye and demanded, "What the fuck is going on with you? Why the fuck are you saying this line? What the fuck is really happening? How the fuck are you feeling, and why? I want you to ask yourself . . . WHY!?" He didn't wait for an answer. He scrambled back over me and out of the car, slammed the door, ran to his camera, and called *"Action!"*

I sat there in shock, in my punk getup and fake Mohawk, wondering what the hell had just happened. He certainly got my attention . . . and a genuine reaction. I had never met a director like Jim before. The two of us really connected on that show. He energized me and inspired me—so much so that years later, on *90210*, I recommended that he come and direct an episode. One episode became eleven episodes, and we worked together for years. I even got Jim to act in an episode I was directing. He was a talented and all-around good guy.

Shooting that episode of *21 Jump Street* was one of most fun weeks of my life. I became friendly with Johnny and his stand-in, Bruce Corkham. Johnny was at a great place in his career—a young star on the rise, for sure, dating another rising star, the stunningly beautiful Sherilyn Fenn. His fame was still quite new and he was still able to walk around Vancouver and live normally without being mobbed or needing security. He definitely had that 1980s bad-boy look down to a tee: off the set he always dressed in jeans, a black leather jacket, a bandanna, and combat boots.

Johnny was not a guy who talked much, but he had some good stories when he got going. He had recently finished shooting *Platoon*, where he'd been basically one of the "kids" on the set observing Tom Berenger and Willem Dafoe. He told us all about how exotic shooting in the Philippines had been, how hot and tropical the weather. As another "kid," for real, I couldn't get enough of these work stories.

The week was tiring, as we shot all night and then I headed off to class every morning, but no sleep was a small price to pay. I soon learned that Holly had a boyfriend—of course she did—but that was okay for now. I had to return to high school.

Downtown Vancouver V6J 5L1

I made several trips down to Los Angeles to see Frank Levy. Frank was a producer as well as a manager. He had visited Vancouver during the winter of 1986 to produce a movie starring Ed Asner, a family Christmas film in which Ed played Santa Claus.

"Kid, you've got something," he had told me. "Come out to L.A. and I'll introduce you to some people. If you move to L.A., you can take a real shot at becoming an actor." He had a special corporate rate for his clients to stay at the Beverly Garland Hotel . . . I think it was $69 a night.

I went on some auditions and met with some of the agents Frank recommended. The reception was good. Frank and I made serious plans for my move as soon as I finished school. If there was one thing I loved about Los Angeles, it was the weather. If there was one thing that surprised me, it was how spread out the city was. Immediately after graduation ceremonies, it was time to move to L.A. But first I had one more acting job—another guest appearance on *21 Jump Street*.

Vancouver in those days was a very small town, acting-wise. Every young person in the business passed through the *21 Jump Street* set at one point or another. This episode was about the perils of underage drinking—in particular, teenage drunk-driving accidents. I played a cool high school kid with a truly impressive mullet. Pauly Shore ap-

peared in a featured role as a hard-partying teenager named TJ, dancing around a table in a bar waving a pool cue.

Holly and I did not have any scenes together, but I found out that
she no longer had a boyfriend. On the set she gave me her number and
casually said that I should give her a call sometime. Holly was twenty-
two and I was seventeen. I was beyond psyched. I called; we set a date,
and on the appointed night I rode my motorcycle downtown and met
her for dinner. One date and I was hooked. I could not wait to see her
again.

We had a couple more dates and I was falling hard, but the new life
that I'd spent the past two years preparing for was beckoning. I sold
my bike, packed up my possessions, and boarded a plane to L.A. It
was time to see what I was made of.

Hollywood
90068

Seventeen years old, a brand-new high school diploma in my back pocket, and raring to go. No more room at the Beverly Garland Hotel for me; I was a resident, not a visitor! My manager, Frank, helped set me up in a small place in Oakwood Gardens on Barham Boulevard, an apartment complex where all the newly single dads and out-of-work actors in L.A. came to live. Another young actor from Canada whom Frank managed, Paul Johansson, was also renting there, so at least I had one friend in the building.

Frank himself lived only a couple of miles away but a world apart from our drab housing. His house was in a gorgeous part of Toluca Lake, filled with tasteful, beautiful homes on large grassy lots. Kids rode bikes and frolicked with their dogs on perfect green lawns in what could have easily passed as a movie set for the ideal American neighborhood. I marveled at the beautiful suburban neighborhoods in the San Fernando Valley and the endless sunshine.

I found an iffy car rental place way out in the Valley that was happy to rent a car to a seventeen-year-old Canadian kid. My red Yugo cost something like $19 a week, so I was happy with it, and my new place was fine. I didn't spend a whole lot of time at home anyway. My first couple of weeks I spent quite a few nights on the phone with Holly, who kept asking, "When are you coming back to Vancouver?" After one of these calls, I dialed her back and said, "Fuck it, I'm coming this weekend." I could not wait another second to see her again. I bought a plane ticket and headed back to my hometown.

When I landed at the airport, Holly picked me up in a shiny red Porsche 944 that was as dazzling as her smile. I jumped in with my overnight bag, and we headed to the charming turn-of-the-century Georgian house she rented in Shaughnessy. There had been plenty of buildup on our phone calls. There wasn't much talking that weekend, but we got to know each other intimately. I never wanted to leave. But come Monday morning she had to be on set, and I had to return to L.A. to try to find a job. The irony that I had lived in Vancouver my entire life was not lost on me. But what the hell . . . I began flying back to see her as often as I possibly could. That's what you do when you're young: buy plane tickets when you don't have any money, fly three hours to see your girl for one night, then turn around and fly right back to L.A., smiling the whole time. Why wouldn't I do that every chance I got?

Luckily, Holly came home to L.A. as often as she could. Her schedule on *21 Jump Street* allowed her to spend a decent amount of time in Los Angeles. Right from the start I was seriously overmatched . . . what was I thinking? Holly was five years older; a beautiful, accomplished young woman who had lived in Paris and worked all over the world. She was interested in a relationship with me? I was like a deer in the headlights. I gave it my best shot, believe me. What I lacked in knowledge and experience I certainly made up for in enthusiasm.

Holly's mother, Dolores, a talent manager, and her brother, Matt, probably wondered about Holly's unusual choice for a boyfriend, but they were gracious and wonderful people who immediately embraced me. Holly and her mom had just bought a house in a Beverly Hills–adjacent neighborhood that needed some fixing up. I headed over there on weekends to help them remodel and paint. The Robinsons welcomed me into their family, pretty much, and for a Canadian kid newly dumped in Los Angeles, the friendship and warmth they offered was invaluable.

Sometimes, conveniently for our romance, I had to return to work in Vancouver. In the fall of 1987, I booked an episode of *MacGyver* there. The star, Richard Dean Anderson, was a delightful guy; originally from Minnesota, he remained very down-to-earth despite the popularity of the show. He was ridiculously handsome—the George Clooney of his day. He was the hottest star on television, never married, who dated an endless string of models and actresses, each more stunning than the last. Still, no one managed to tie him down. He had charm to spare plus a great sense of humor about the show and the way his character was always able to save the day with a book of matches and a pipe cleaner . . . or whatever he happened to have on hand that week.

Once again, I arrived on set to find my old friend Bernie. We were cast as best friends, the teenage sons of MacGyver's childhood friends. In our episode, entitled "Blood Brothers," Bernie got in way over his head with drugs, and gang members came after him. I played the loyal friend who tried to help and took a bullet for my efforts—though MacGyver saved me in the end, of course. "Dude, tell me what you're doing!" Bernie said the minute we had time to talk.

"Living in L.A., man!"

"Oh, man," he said. "I need to be in L.A.!" My old friend was doing quite well for himself. I wasn't surprised; he was an immensely talented actor. He had just shot a key role in Jodie Foster's movie *The Accused* as the haunted witness to her vicious gang rape. But Bernie could be erratic. He showed up four hours late one day to the set, with his hair dyed a different color and a ring in his nose, looking like he'd slept outside all night (he probably had). The producers were not pleased at the delays this caused as the makeup department frantically bleached his hair back to its regular blond shade and tried to fill in the hole in his nose.

Naturally, he emerged from the trailer to do brilliant work. He was absolutely amazing once the cameras rolled that day, so all was forgiven. Plus, he was truly remorseful. I was bemused by his behavior, but it was just one day and he'd quickly redeemed himself, so I shook my head for a minute and forgot about it. As shooting wrapped we talked about our futures, and Bernie made a snap decision.

"Let's go back together—we'll take my car! I just bought a Caddy! Let's go in that! I'll drive." Bernie had no driver's license, but he did somehow own a huge beast of a Cadillac. That was very Bernie. I cashed in my return plane ticket and bought some gas.

"We're going to Hollywood in my Coupe de Ville!" Oh, that car: a harvest gold 1967 Coupe de Ville with a vinyl top. It was gigantic. The backseat was longer and wider than most beds; we took turns resting back there on a few brief breaks. The shocks were blown. The stereo—and by stereo I mean the cassette player—was tied up with a hockey skate lace, swinging under the dashboard. We blasted Elvis Costello tapes all the way to L.A. and drove straight through. Coffee and NoDoz, coffee and more NoDoz. It was an epic road trip, twenty hours straight, ending triumphantly at my friend Dave Sherrill's pad in North Hollywood. The Canadians had arrived to take over L.A.!

North Hollywood 91601

Bernie and I rented an apartment together at 5050 Klump Avenue in North Hollywood: your basic Valley craphole. We were super-excited about living together and about our new lives in L.A.

For the next six or eight months, my life became a routine of living in L.A. and auditioning for roles, running out of money, then getting offered jobs back in Canada, taking them, getting paid, coming back and living in L.A. . . . and on and on it went . . .

One night, I returned to our apartment after a long-delayed flight from Vancouver where I was shooting *Danger Bay*. I was tired and wanted to rest, but when I walked into my room, I found some random guy asleep in my bed.

"Bernie!" I yelled. I went back out in the living room, where my roommate was crashed on the sofa. This is where he could generally be found unless he was working. "Wanna tell me who that tall skinny guy in my bed might be?"

"Oh right, dude. That's Brad. He's been staying here while you were gone, but he's a really cool guy—an actor, you'll like him."

The stranger woke up and came wandering out, half asleep. "Hey, man, we didn't know you'd be back. Sorry about this." Brad Pitt was the nicest midwestern guy imaginable. We became fast friends, and suddenly the three of us were living in our two-bedroom craphole apartment. Brad slept on the couch and looked for a more permanent place to live. We lived on Ramen noodles and generic beer—the kind that came in white cans labeled BEER—and Marlboro Light cigarettes. We were all broke.

We didn't even own a television set! Our "entertainment system" was an ancient Akai boom box with some cassette tapes scattered around, and a keyboard Bernie liked to tinker with and make music. Just for fun, we used to have competitions over who could go the longest without showering and shaving. Brad always won. Having to go on an audition meant cleaning up, which is what usually put an end to the streak.

One of our favorite pastimes was to get into Brad's car—a crappy blue Nissan 200SX he fondly called Runaround Sue—and strap on our seat belts. "Seatbelt Dummies" was the name of the game. This was back in the days before airbags. We'd drive around looking for things to crash into . . . Dumpsters were ideal, because they rolled slightly. The idea was to go flying forward with as much force as possible until the strap at your waist jerked you back, practically cutting you in half. We wouldn't crash into anything that hard . . . but certainly Runaround Sue's front end had a lot of dents in it. It was the funniest thing ever. All the guys we hung out with—a loose group of mostly unemployed actors—loved it.

Can you tell that it was a much easier and simpler time, the late '80s? Brad and Bernie and me, running around Hollywood with the cool stonewashed jeans and the big feathered hair. Things were very different then in the dating world; everyone kept their lives much more compartmentalized. There wasn't a lot of group socializing. You hung with your boys, the girls hung with their girls, and couples went out on dates by themselves. No one was particularly anxious to mix.

I was perfectly happy hanging out with my crew; otherwise, I went on auditions and spent every minute I could with Holly. Brad eventually landed a role on *Head of the Class* and had a brief fling with Robin Givens, who'd recently left her husband, Mike Tyson, in a blaze of headlines. Bernie, who was still involved with a girl from Vancouver, Lisa Wolverton, appeared in a movie with Patrick Dempsey about a pizza guy, then in another movie with Jason Bateman. Those early days in L.A. when we were broke, just scraping together enough money to stay in L.A., were a great time in my life.

With my limited budget, I happily accepted an offer from the Robinsons to join them in Tahiti for Christmas of 1987. All the Robinsons were going; they had rented several bungalows for everyone to stay in, so all I had to do was buy my plane ticket. The tropical setting was magical, but it did not turn out to be the dream trip we had all envisioned. We were riding around the island on rented scooters one hot afternoon when Holly's mother, Dolores, crashed. She had to be rushed to the hospital and have immediate surgery on her foot. Fortunately, she was fine, but the incident threw a pall over the vacation. It was an omen. It was becoming clear that Holly and I would soon part ways.

When we returned home from Tahiti after New Year's Day 1988, it was clear the relationship had run its course. Like many breakups, it wasn't totally clean and over with one discussion; there was a bit of back and forth, and some anguished discussions and second thoughts, but the romance soon had come to an end. As of course it was destined . . . I was eighteen years old; we weren't going to stay together forever. There were certainly more suitable mates on her horizon as well.

Though the romance was over, Holly meant too much to me in every way to lose touch. We salvaged a friendship out of what had been a sweet youthful fling and have remained friends to this day. Holly is a beautiful, sophisticated woman, and she set the bar very high in terms of romantic relationships. I could not have asked for a more idyllic first love.

Vancouver
V5K 2H9

Brad came home one day and said, "Hey, I found a little house for rent over on La Jolla in West Hollywood; right across the street from the Comedy Store. I'm going to move there; it's a two-bedroom place if either of you want to move in."

Bernie looked at me and said, "Jason. Whattaya wanna do?"

I said, "You take it. I'm going back to Vancouver."

The writers' strike of 1988 was upon us. The main disagreements between the writers and producers included residuals for hour-long shows and expanded creative rights the writers were demanding (like the choice of actors and directors for some projects). The strike would last for 155 days and bring the industry to a standstill. There would be no production. Hollywood would be shut down.

There would be work in Canada, though, and there was nothing keeping me in L.A. So I packed my bags, wished Bernie and Brad well, and bought a ticket home.

When I got to Vancouver, I reached out to my old friend Bruce Corkham to see if I could crash at his place for a bit until I figured out what my living situation would be. He told me he and his roommate, Sam, had an extra room that I could have and we could all split the rent.

"Perfect," I said. And I moved in.

I soon learned that living with two guys from Halifax means living with everyone they've ever known from Halifax. Maritimers are legendary for their hospitality. And Bruce and Sam were no exception.

One day I came home in the middle of the afternoon to find a girl sitting at our kitchen table, drinking my whiskey.

"Hi," I said. "Who are you?"

"I'm Sarah," she said.

"So, Sarah, why are you drinking my whiskey?" I asked.

"Oh. Hey. I didn't know this was yours," she said. "Sorry about that."

"No problem, but maybe you could pour me some." I pulled up a chair. We started talking and she told me she was a musician, a singer specifically, visiting from Halifax to find a manager. She was looking to further her music career in Vancouver, because that's where everything was really happening. And they did go on to happen for her, in a big way. Her first album, *Touch,* would appear a year later. I have stayed in touch with Sarah McLachlan ever since, following her happily as her concert venues grew bigger and bigger, and am delighted to say she is still a friend of mine today.

I was working pretty steadily in Canada, but the writers' strike seemed to be coming to an end in L.A. Finally, my agent called me and said, "I've got a movie offer for you! But you have to work as a local and get yourself a work permit. I've got the name and number of an attorney who can work this out for you, but you've got to come now. I mean, right now. Jump on a plane."

I called my buddy Dave Sherrill to see if I could stay with him for a month, immediately flew down to L.A., and went back to that shady car rental place and got that same red Yugo for $19 a week. I went to see a very high-powered immigration attorney in Century City, and he made the work permit happen.

Temptation Blues, or *Nowhere to Run,* as it was called when it was finally released, starred David Carradine, the actor and martial artist who was newly sober at the time and still a bit fragile. The movie was set in 1960 in rural Texas, and David spent a lot of time wandering around the set with a gun over his shoulder. It wasn't a great film; the tagline was "Hot-Blooded Teenagers . . . Cold-Blooded Murder." I played one of a bunch of high school seniors with a terrible secret. In real life, David had no teeth—they had been kicked out by a horse if I remember correctly—and he kept his new teeth in his front shirt pocket. He never put them in when he was relaxing off-camera or rehearsing.

We'd go over our lines once or twice, and when it was time to take our places, he'd say to the director, "Yeah, we gonna shoot this one? If so, I'm gonna put my teeth in." He'd pull his teeth from his pocket, pop them into his mouth, and say, "All right, I'm ready to go." It was hysterical. I didn't mind that he was a little crazy; this was *David Carradine,* the legendary kung fu star. It's characters like him that make this business great. He was truly larger than life.

But that movie ended. As they all do. And I had to figure out what my next step was going to be. I didn't know it then, but the next three months would change my life forever.

The Valley
91523

A month of sleeping on Dave's sofa had not only given me an appreciation for a good bed, his roommates' cats had given me scabies. I didn't even know what scabies were. I'd never even heard of them. But I can tell you, they were not fun. The ugly, itchy skin rashes were not what any actor wants to show up with at an audition.

One day, Dave said to me, "Let's take a drive."

I said, "Okay."

We headed north on 101. Dave asked me, "So what are you going to do now that the movie is done?"

"I don't know. . . . Head back to Vancouver, I guess," I replied.

"You can't go back there, Jason."

"What do you mean? Why not?"

"Because you're here! Why would you ever go backward? You've got your papers for a few months, so stay. This is where it's at! Bank on your success! You need to bet on yourself succeeding. You will make it here, Jason. Don't go back to Vancouver."

I listened to what he said.

"Look, I'm gonna move out of that place. Let's get a place together. We'll be roommates. You have to count on success."

I knew Dave was right. I just needed to hear it. Obviously, I said yes, and Dave and I started to look for a cat-free apartment that very day. And we found one. In Malibu Canyon.

I owe a lot to Dave Sherrill. He was a great friend to me early in my career. And as he was older than I, he was a great teacher in many ways. Had Dave and I not had that talk in his car that day, I would have returned to Vancouver and the same busy career I was enjoying. But that was nothing compared to what was on the horizon for me in L.A.

Van Nuys
91401

Like many actors who appear to burst on the scene out of nowhere, it took me a good ten years to become an "overnight success." Meanwhile, it was audition, audition, audition. Hustle, hustle, hustle. And broke, broke, broke. I had turned in my rented Yugo and bought a used Honda Interceptor 500 motorcycle with my movie money, promptly racking up parking tickets all over the Valley, plus a speeding ticket one day on a canyon road.

Naturally, I forgot all about my speeding ticket, thinking it was no big deal and I'd take care of it . . . sometime. Eventually, it went into warrant status. I was driving around Laurel Canyon one afternoon, going to visit some girl, when I ran out of gas. This was a not-infrequent occurrence, because I rarely had the cash to put more than five or six dollars' worth of gas in at a time. As I pushed my bike up the road to the gas station ahead, a cop car came up behind me. I was happy to see him—I thought he might help me. "Hey, Officer, I ran out of gas. I'm just pushing this down to the gas station," I told him.

"You go ahead and push it down to the station. Then you're going to lock it up and come with me. I just ran your plates, and there's a warrant out for your arrest, Mr. Priestley."

I nearly fell over. "What? Hold on!"

"Let's move it," he said. All was explained down at the gas station.

At least the cop didn't confiscate my bike; he let me lock it up and took me to the Van Nuys jail, where I languished in a waiting room. I had one phone call, so I called my roommate, Dave. With all the overdue fines, penalties, and interest, it was going to cost $283 to get out, a sum that nearly killed me. Dave showed up with three hundred bucks and bailed me out. We then returned to the station, picked up my bike, and filled it with gas. I paid him back with what little money I had in the bank. That was one expensive trip, and I never even saw the girl!

In those days the Sunset Strip was very much geared to the heavy metal rockers. Guns N' Roses and Ratt ruled. All the girls who wanted to hang out with the rocker guys followed them to West Hollywood. Big hair, black leather, spandex . . . that was the look on the Strip at the time. My friends and I weren't those guys; we hung out in Hollywood. We used to drink for cheap at the Sunset Social Club and the Dresden Room. Sometimes we'd go to Prince's club downtown, the Glam Slam, to dance and drink all night. Other nights we would just hang out at the duplex or drive around playing Seatbelt Dummies, which never failed to amuse us.

There was plenty of fun and good times, but work always came first for me. I was out there auditioning every day. I had work papers that were good for a few months, and I needed to beat that ticking clock. I was working hard every night preparing material, then auditioning the next day. I was getting multiple callbacks. The energy was flowing. I was on the cusp of something big . . . I could just feel it.

Burbank
91523

After a long run on *Dynasty* and *The Colbys,* Stephanie Beacham was shooting a new pilot for NBC called *Sister Kate.* Around the same time I auditioned for the lead in a Disney Channel miniseries called *Teen Angel.* I was on my third callback for *Sister Kate* when I got the news that I'd won the role on *Teen Angel.*

This marked the true turning point in my career; at nineteen, *Teen Angel* was the "big break" I'd been waiting for. Disney had high hopes for this movie; they were really hoping it would be a hit and spawn some sequels. It was in their best interest to ensure that I'd be around in the future. By taking this role, I got a three-year work permit, a huge break for me. Shooting began at once and I was needed on set immediately, so I left right away for location in Arizona.

I played the "teen angel" of the title, a young guy named Buzz Gunderson who had been killed in the late 1950s and had been waiting nearly thirty years for his first assignment. Buzz was sent back to Earth to be the guardian angel for another teenager, a kid named Dennis, who was enamored of the '50s lifestyle. Adam Biesk was my costar. The girl with the lead role was a teenager named Renee O'Connor; she would later become very well known on *Xena: Warrior Princess.*

With acting, it's either feast or famine, so naturally in the middle of shooting *Teen Angel,* the call came in to my agent from *Sister Kate.* The network wanted me back for one absolute last, final audition for the top brass at NBC. We were night shooting at the time, so the producers tinkered a bit with my schedule and arranged it so I could shoot all night and then hop on the first flight from Phoenix for the one-hour flight trip back to Los Angeles the next morning.

I needed a ride from the Burbank airport over to NBC for the final test. Dave was on location shooting a movie, so I called Brad, the only other friend I had who was responsible enough to actually pick me up when he said he would. Sure enough, he met me at the airport in trusty Runaround Sue, drove me to NBC, and waited during my meeting. The audition went really well; after my final test, they told me I got the part right then and there. I went downstairs and gave Brad the good news. The two of us immediately headed out to celebrate.

We pulled into the parking lot of the closest bar we could find, a place called Dalt's. At that time the area was still full of lots of little mom-and-pop establishments: stores, restaurants, neighborhood bars for the locals. Now, of course, it's the heart of downtown Burbank, full of big corporate office buildings with upscale chain restaurants like Morton's and McCormick & Schmick's as the anchor tenants on their ground floors.

The bar was cool and dark and quiet in the late morning. Brad and I sat at the bar and did one celebratory shot, toasting to my success. It was great to have a buddy who was genuinely happy for me. Then it was back to work. He dropped me off at the airport, and I hopped a plane back to Phoenix to finish the shoot.

The assistant director on *Teen Angel* was a British guy who was returning to England as soon as production wrapped. He drove a very cool Alfa Romeo Milano that I loved. "Hey, Jason, I have to go back home. I'm going to turn in my car," he told me. "Unless you want to take over the lease?" I said sure and took over his lease. This was quite a step up from my Honda Interceptor, or Bernie's Coupe de

Ville that I occasionally drove. Definitely a step up from the rented Yugo. Bernie usually didn't drive, as he couldn't be bothered to get a license or insurance—again, very Bernie. We drove him to his auditions, or if no one was available, he would drive himself.

I had one show wrapped, a pilot coming up, and a blue Alfa Romeo Milano.

Salt Lake City
84103

Stephanie Beacham was certainly the hottest nun I'd ever seen. In the *Sister Kate* pilot she played a brisk, no-nonsense nun who was put in charge of a bunch of orphans at a Catholic home called Redemption House. Besides being beautiful, Stephanie was funny and charming and an incredibly talented actress. She was just coming off a highly successful run as Sable on *The Colbys* and had decided to take a chance on a very different kind of show. Instead of a glamorous role on an Aaron Spelling nighttime soap, she'd be the star of a standard sitcom surrounded by a whole bunch of kids.

Right after I shot the pilot, I got some good news: *Teen Angel* had done well enough in the ratings to merit a sequel. I flew out to Salt Lake City for the shoot.

I was fooling around just before I left and for some reason punched a wall. No real reason, just doing stupid shit like young guys do. I wound up with a boxer's fracture, which the doctor wanted to put in a cast. I couldn't do that, because I was leaving the next day to shoot *Teen Angel Returns*.

"Come on," I told the skeptical doctor. "I'm leaving for Salt Lake City to shoot a movie. I can't have my hand in a cast!"

He shook his head but gave me a removable cast with Velcro fastenings to wear whenever I was off-camera. Unfortunately for me, *Teen Angel*'s Buzz was a very active guy. I had to jump in and out of cars and do all sorts of minor stunts, all of which were agony. I could barely even drive my own car with its stick shift.

Still, the cast gave me a bit of a bad-boy aura, which was fine with me. That was what was cool at the time—everyone wanted to be bad. Smoking, drinking, sullen expression like you were sucking a lemon, filthy ripped jeans . . . that was the look of the day. Girls liked "bad boys." As far as girls were concerned, no one could ever say I liked a particular "type"—I liked all kinds! There were some cute girls on this set, including a blonde named Jennie Garth, who played the lead's friend. But as soon as I laid eyes on Robyn, it was all over.

Robyn Lively had reddish curls, sparkly brown eyes, and freckles sprinkled over an adorable face. A couple of years younger than I, she still lived at home with her parents in Northridge and was doing quite well with her own acting career. It was the oldest story in the world: Robyn was dating Rick Schroeder, whom she'd met on *Silver Spoons,* when she and I hooked up on location in Salt Lake City. You know the story: young actors, working together, away from home . . . one thing most definitely led to another. Our clandestine little affair was going great until Rick stopped by for a visit. I was on the outs with Robyn for a few days when Rick rolled into town, but after he took off, I was back in. It was all very cloak-and-dagger.

Soon enough, of course, we all returned home to L.A., where Robyn and I continued to see each other in secret. Rick was no fool; he had sensed something going on in Salt Lake City. Rick was friendly with my roommate, Dave; the two of them had worked together in the past. Next thing I knew, Rick started coming by the house, oh so casually, supposedly to see Dave. "Hey, Dave, what's going on, man? Thought I'd drop by and see what was happening." And then . . . "Oh, Jason. *You* live here?" Surprised look. "You guys are roommates? That's awesome." It was so transparent. There was some sneaking around, some hiding of cars, and even during one particularly close call, a night when Robyn had to hide in the closet. Dave was not happy.

"Dude. This is not cool," he would tell me every few days. "This can't be going on here in our apartment. You guys gotta deal with this, man. Tell him. This is so not cool!" Dave was a laid-back surfer kind of guy; he didn't want any drama. The other thing was, Rick was a good guy, and I liked him.

The situation was all quite highly charged for a while, until Robyn came clean to Rick in a big cathartic scene—which I was nowhere near. When all the dust had settled, Robyn and I emerged as an official couple. What more can I say? We were so young, and it all meant so much at the time.

Prospect Studios
Los Feliz
90027

The *Sister Kate* pilot aired in September of 1989. Next thing I knew, the show was picked up and I was headed to New York for the upfronts to promote the show. Being part of the upfronts—the lavish preview of their season's offerings networks put on for advertisers, press, and critics—marked a whole new level for me in terms of career advancement.

Stephanie Beacham and I, along with one of the younger kids and some production staff, sat in a hotel suite on the day of our appearance waiting to be briefed. I was beyond thrilled to be there. Brandon Tartikoff and Warren Littlefield were running NBC at the time, and I was awed by their programming genius. Under their stewardship, NBC was an absolute ratings juggernaut. Nobody could touch them for years and years. I was truly humbled by this opportunity and determined to make the most of it.

The executives arrived to fill us in on what was happening that day, what to expect when we made our appearance, talking points to mention to the press, their hopes for the show—just general background preparation that I, for one, greatly appreciated. I was happy just to be in the presence of these guys. These powerful, intelligent, game-changing executives really were changing the face of TV.

Life could not have been better. In addition to a new apartment and a role on a network series lined up, Robyn and I were living out a true storybook romance. Everything just clicked; we were a perfect fit. Our ages were compatible: I was twenty to her eighteen. She was a talented actress, working on series like *Twin Peaks* and *Doogie Howser, M.D.* She had come from Powder Springs, Georgia, originally, a real girlie-girl who was ultraromantic. She wanted to do things like exchange cards on our anniversary every month. My friends all loved her too; they thought she was just a doll. Dave, Brad, all the guys—without exception, every friend I had said to me, "That girl's a keeper." Believe me, I knew it.

Robyn's parents were good people. She lived at home the whole time we dated, so I got to know her mother and stepfather quite well. Robyn's stepfather, Ernie, was a former actor who ran a highly regarded acting school. Both he and her mom, Elaine, liked me, and I liked hanging out with the family and their adorable baby daughter, Blake. It was clear I was crazy about their older daughter. Why wouldn't I be . . . she was beautiful, smart, and successful. Truly, we should have starred in a teenage love movie, as our relationship was everything that young love should be.

Sister Kate was filmed at the ABC lot on Prospect, directly across the hall from *Mr. Belvedere,* a popular show about a proper British butler living with a typical American family. The two shows shared the same writers and show runners. I kept my head down, did everything I was asked with a smile on my face, and tried to show I was a team player.

Sister Kate was my first big multicamera, American-style sitcom, and I learned how to deliver a very specific kind of sitcom comedy. The experience was invaluable; not to mention, it was fun. Stephanie was wonderful to work with, and we were glad to have each other as we were the only two adults on the show. Everyone else in the cast was a young kid . . . meaning stage parents galore!

When I was a kid actor, my mom used to drop me off on the set and pick me up at the end of the day—that's what people did in the

1970s. I had never seen the kind of nonsense some of these parents were pulling on little kids. To be fair, I saw both ends of the spectrum: kind, loving parents who were there because acting was their kid's dream, and they were on set to support them every step of the way. Then there was the other, much more disturbing kind of parent: adults pushing their kids mercilessly when it was clear who really dreamed of an acting career.

The kids on the show could, by law, only work eight hours a day, so the producers would send them all home at the end of the day. Stephanie and I would stay late at night, and the writers would quickly rewrite anything that wasn't working with the kids so that Stephanie and I had their lines instead and we could get those scenes shot that night.

The two of us spent many a Friday night together: one A.M., the audience long gone, the two of us shooting scenes that had just been written, tons of new dialogue. Most of the main scenes on that show were shot in the kitchen, so we used to frantically handwrite our dialogue on the cabinets behind each other in pencil. That way, instead of looking each other in the face, we could look just beyond each other's head and read our dialogue off the cabinets in the background. There was no way we could have memorized it in the sixty seconds since they handed us the new pages. It was a great time.

For a Halloween episode on the show I dressed up in a nun's habit just like hers. In the scene Stephanie came down the stairs and walked right up to me; we stood there in identical habits, face-to-face. She stared right at me and burst out, "I thought I was the pretty one!" The live audience loved it; they were laughing and cheering and clapping. There were lots of funny moments and cool guest stars. Still, it wasn't enough.

Stephanie's gamble on a broad comedy with kids unfortunately didn't pay off the way we all hoped. *Sister Kate* had a good run for nineteen episodes, but after the first season it was very clear we were on life support. In addition to the invaluable sitcom experience, the show was a financial bonanza for me. I had banked every paycheck without even touching it. It was time to look for my own place.

The Lot and FOX Studios
Century City
90046

Although I was still officially under contract to NBC, it was clear that *Sister Kate* was not going to be renewed. My agent, Nick, had been looking around to see what else might be out there. He called me one Wednesday afternoon in the middle of pilot season. "Aaron Spelling is doing a new show and I've got the script for the pilot. Read it and see what you think. It's okay, nothing really special, but because it is Aaron you should probably take a look."

"What's it about?"

"Family moves from the Midwest to L.A. and their two kids have to start over at Beverly Hills High School. All the roles are cast except for this one: the lead guy who plays the son. The production's ready to go; in fact, they start shooting on Monday, but they've got to lock this last role down. Immediately."

"This Monday? Wow."

"I'm messengering this to your house right now; give it a read and call me tonight."

I read the script and agreed with Nick's assessment—it was okay. Brandon was definitely a role I should at least audition for. I was now twenty, but in TV world could still easily play high school, or fifteen, as Brandon was supposed to be. Nick had set up a meeting for the next afternoon at Spelling Productions. We spoke briefly that night about the script. "Go get it!" he said. I worked on my material late into the night.

I drove over to the Lot studio, a small, obscure location on Santa Monica and Formosa, and walked over to Aaron Spelling Productions. I checked in and then took a seat in the waiting room of Aaron's private office. I was surrounded by every other young actor in town, most of whom I knew from chasing other roles. *Everybody's here,* I realized. Crap. Pilot season, a new Spelling show—the competition was stiff.

My name was eventually called and I stood at the huge oak door that opened into Aaron's inner sanctum. It was at least fifteen feet tall with ornate brass handles. I took a deep breath, pushed open the heavy door, and immediately stepped into the deepest shag carpeting I'd ever seen in my life. Seriously, I was buried nearly to my ankles. The office was huge. A dark-haired girl was sitting with a man on a long white built-in couch that took up an entire wall on one side of the office; Aaron himself was pouring a tumbler of vodka at the full bar set up in another corner. *Charlie's Angels* and *Dynasty* posters covered the walls. The room was the epitome of '70s chic decor, though it was 1990. I had never seen anything like it in my life.

The man on the couch, who turned out to be a casting director, jumped up and introduced me. "Jason, this is Mr. Spelling; Mr. Spelling, Jason Priestley." Drink in hand, Aaron shuffled over to shake my hand. I was dazzled by meeting the television legend in person in his over-the-top office and did my best to imprint the whole scene on my brain. Aaron and I walked over to the couch together and Aaron said, "Jason . . . this is Shannen, she's our Brenda."

"Nice to meet you," I said. She nodded.

"So . . . how'd you like to read a few scenes together for us?" Aaron asked. I sat down, we read a few short scenes together, and it seemed to go well; there was decent chemistry between us. When we finished, Aaron said, "Great, Jason, great . . . tell me . . . do you think you could make it over to FOX tomorrow for a network reading?"

"I could probably squeeze that in for you, Aaron," I said. He smiled. He got the joke.

"Good, good . . ." he said. "We'll have you do these same scenes for the people over there . . . I'll see you then." I said my thank-yous and exited. There were still eight or ten guys waiting to be seen, but I had at least made it to the next round.

I jumped into my Alfa Romeo and raced home. The phone was ringing as I walked in the door. Nick was calling to hammer out my deal points. All actor deals are struck before you go to the network for a final test, so that no one can hold the production up for more money should the pilot lead to a hit show. My contract was prenegotiated then and there for five years. (Nowadays, it's usually seven.)

The next day, Friday, I dressed in a different T-shirt but kept the jeans and tennis shoes (that's what we all wore back then). I drove to the network meeting on the FOX lot, where I sat in a different waiting room with the other two final contenders. One of the guys I knew by sight, just seeing him around auditions, and one of the guys I didn't. None of us spoke.

When it was my turn, I entered the office and Aaron himself greeted me. He pulled me aside to a corner of the office. From inside his jacket he pulled a page torn out of a recent *People* magazine; it was a small column item about me on *Sister Kate*. "I just showed this to everyone," he whispered. "Don't worry—I'm looking out for you." He winked and clapped me on the back.

Then he took me over to meet everybody—including Barry Diller, FOX's chairman and CEO. Shannen wasn't there so I read with the casting director. My audition seemed to go well enough and once again I said my thank-yous and left.

I have no idea what Aaron did or said once I left the room, but he wasn't kidding about being in my corner. Late that afternoon I had the role, along with an invitation. Everyone in the cast was gathering at Aaron's home Sunday night for a table read. It was time to meet my "classmates."

Bel Air
90077

The Spellings had not yet built their famous fifty-six-thousand-square-foot "Manor," and the family lived in a large, beautiful but still regular-sized home. Regular-sized for Bel Air. The new cast all gathered in the huge living room that featured more shag carpeting. That man loved his shag carpeting. There were crystal ashtrays and holders full of cigarettes all over the place; a slight haze of smoke in the air; beautiful paintings and luxurious furnishings. It was just fantastic. I was in somewhat of a daze, knowing that the very next morning I would be reporting to the set to star in a pilot. It had all happened very quickly.

I was happily surprised to see Jennie Garth again—a perfect choice for the stuck-up rich girl she was going to play. Shannen I had already met, and I was sure we could work well together in the brother/sister relationship we would have on the show. Ian Ziering was the embodiment of the Beverly Hills jock, and Brian Austin Green and Tori, Aaron's daughter, seemed much younger than the rest of the cast; they were both actually still in high school at the time. They really were the geeky little kids looking on with wide eyes! Everyone was friendly, happy, and excited about this new project.

We did a quick read-through of the script, and the chemistry was strong and immediate. Everyone started riffing as soon as we began reading the script, playing off each other, and the banter all went so smoothly. Any show runner will tell you . . . casting is nine-tenths of the battle. If you can assemble the right group of people, it's like catching lightning in a bottle. Everything sure felt right. We broke up early with everyone feeling happy and optimistic.

A mile or so away from the house, I was heading east on Sunset Boulevard and glanced to my right to see Gabrielle Carteris driving in her rental car. She was from New York and rarely drove. She was sitting with her back ramrod straight, hands clenched tightly on the wheel, looking neither to the right or the left. She was clearly absolutely terrified to be driving down winding Sunset Boulevard. I, of course, was racing full speed, cigarette going, stereo blasting. I took one more look and had to shake my head at Aaron's genius. *Where did they find that girl?* I wondered. *She is an absolutely perfect shy and timid Andrea!*

I gunned the engine and pulled away in my Alfa Romeo. I had a 6:30 call to be fitted for wardrobe the next morning. I could feel it in the air; something new and big was coming down the line. My life was about to change forever—and I wanted to be ready for it.

FOX Private Jet
New York
10019

We shot the pilot over the next two weeks. As is often the case, the pilot was somewhat different from what the actual show would become. It had been written by Darren Star and was directed by Tim Hunter, who was an independent film director. He had shot *The River's Edge* starring Keanu Reeves. Because Tim had an indie-film sensibility, the pilot had a slightly darker, moodier feel as opposed to the slick, shiny beautiful-kids-in-beautiful-locations TV show that *90210* would eventually become.

The final product was called *The Class of Beverly Hills*. The show opened with me, as Brandon, lying fast asleep in a bedroom filled with half-unpacked boxes, hitting the alarm as it goes off at 6:30 A.M. As his stereo blasted Brandon awake, he rolled over and said, "First day of school. Strange city. New house. No friends . . . I'm psyched." Then he dropped his head back into the pillow and went back to sleep. Ninety minutes later, after romantic escapades for both Brandon and Brenda, there I was, having a heartfelt talk with Brenda about the great teenage preoccupation: "doing it." The show closed with Brandon lying in the dark, hands behind his head, thinking over their strange new life at West Beverly Hills High.

My reaction to this pilot was basically, "Huh. Well, that was fun," and in my mind I pretty much moved on to the next thing. I thought the pilot was okay, and my performance had been okay, but there was no way that show was going to get picked up. Robyn and I headed off to Hawaii for a quick vacation. I couldn't believe it when just a few weeks later, in May, Nick called to tell me that the show had been picked up. By shooting the pilot, of course, we had all contractually agreed to be in the show if and when it was picked up. I had a new series, a steady job. It was great but surprising news.

The FOX network was still quite new at the time; the so-called fourth network was not even five years old and had plenty to prove. The next step was the upfronts. I had been through this with *Sister Kate,* but I was playing a bigger role this time. Shannen and I were basically the two actors chosen to be paraded in front of all the advertisers to generate interest for our show. We were told to jump on the FOX jet to fly to New York. A number of FOX people, including Jamie Kellner, Brad Turrell, and Sandy Grushow, were on this flight as well.

Now, this new show had just barely been picked up. Shannen and I were not stars. We were both young working actors—period. We were a last-minute addition to the passenger list on this jet, which was carrying major industry executives, including Jamie, the head of the entire FOX network. I could not believe my ears at Shannen's very first words after she boarded. Her butt had barely hit her seat before she said loudly to the PR person, "Really? A town car? You send a town car to take me to the airport, not a limo?" She sighed a very put-upon sigh. I laughed, as I couldn't really tell if Shannen was kidding or not.

But that was just the beginning. I looked on, becoming more uneasy by the minute as she began bitching about the short notice and the food on board and the temperature in the cabin and everything else. I tried to play it off. I laughed like she was joking, then took her arm and dragged her to the back of the plane.

"What are you doing?" I said. Shannen looked at me blankly. "Stop talking. Just sit here for the rest of the flight and be quiet."

I shook my head; I couldn't believe what I was hearing. Meanwhile, she had no idea what my problem was. She honestly could not understand what I was so worried about. It was a long, long flight.

All of us stayed at the Peninsula Hotel on Fifth Avenue, a gorgeous five-star property with every possible amenity. FOX put on an extravagant show for the advertisers. After we completed our duties, both Shannen and I were anxious to go shopping. We had an entire day off before returning to L.A. that night, so I asked a staffer at FOX if we could get a car for a few hours that day to take us around town. The doorman held open the entrance door on Fifth Avenue as Shannen and I headed outside, where we happened to see Brad Terrell waiting for a cab. A shiny black town car was there waiting for us. Perfect.

Shannen glanced at Brad, looked at the car where a uniformed driver was opening the door for her, then turned back to Brad, and said, "Really? Again? A fucking town car? Again, I don't get a limo?" To say I was staggered by the sheer nerve of a nineteen-year-old girl, whose show had just been picked up and had no track record on this network, speaking to our head of PR in this manner would be an understatement. Once again I tried to play it off, smiling at Brad as if to say, *Oh, isn't she a riot.* I put my arm around Shannen and guided her firmly down the stairs to the waiting car. "Get in the car, Shannen," I hissed. This girl was freaking unbelievable. That was the start of four years working closely with Shannen Doherty.

There were many similar rides ahead for me and Shannen, and not all of them were fun. But some of them actually were. Shannen, obviously, also had her good side; she was an amusing and entertaining girl, and we had a lot of good times together. We actually had a blast in New York City that afternoon, once we got going. A large part of her quirky charm was the fact that she really and truly did not give a shit. She would say or do anything. It was a very cool attitude, until it wasn't. I quickly realized that Yugo and town car—in her eyes—were one and the same.

Beverly Hills 90210

Everywhere I looked around me in Beverly Hills were designer boutiques like Cartier, Versace, and Hermès, along with upscale eateries like Mako and hotels like the Beverly Wilshire. The pressure to spend on luxuries was powerful. But I wasn't the kind of guy to throw my first big earnings away on Ferraris and yacht trips; that kind of rock star spending would never be me. My grandfather had been a highly successful Realtor in Canada, and my mother had eventually segued from teaching into real estate as a career. I'd grown up hearing about properties, mortgages, financing, curb appeal, and fixer-uppers, so I probably knew more than the average twenty-year-old about real estate.

I absolutely knew better than to just throw my money away on rent every month; the importance of owning property was ingrained in me. Why pay somebody else's mortgage? For the long haul, in an uncertain career, I needed a permanent place to live. With the money I'd saved from *Sister Kate,* I bought a sensible town house in a desirable area of Sherman Oaks, just south of Ventura Boulevard with its hundreds of shops and restaurants. It was centrally located, about ten minutes away from my new job. Official shooting on *Beverly Hills 90210* began immediately after the Fourth of July holiday that summer of 1990, and I was ready.

It was exciting. I was finally moving into my own place. And it truly was my place; I owned it. I had actually bought my first home at the age of twenty. And I was starting production on my first television series where I was the star—number one on the call sheet. I was working very hard to stay focused and prove to everyone that their belief in me was well founded.

As we prepared to shoot the first episode, called "The Green Room," our executive producer hosted a table read at his house, so we could all get to meet one another and be a little more comfortable before showing up to the first day of work the following day.

I parked my Alfa in the street and walked up to Chuck Rosin's house. There was a guy standing on the front porch . . . the new guy who'd been added since the pilot. I stuck out my hand and said, "Hey, man, I'm Jason." He shook my hand and said, "I'm Luke; I'm playing Dylan."

"Great, great . . . so listen, Luke." He cocked his head. My character, Brandon, was to befriend this mysterious surfer-dude character Dylan. "Do you surf?"

He shook his head. "Nope. Never surfed in my life."

"Good. You and I are going to get along just fine." It was the beginning of a beautiful friendship. Many good times lay ahead in our future.

I FELT AARON SPELLING'S warmth and caring from my very first day on the set, and partly out of respect for him, I took my work very seriously. As number one on the call sheet—meaning the star, the cast member whose name was first in the credits every week—I took ownership of my job, and the show, from day one. Even before we went into production, I walked around the studio talking to the crew members, introducing myself, getting a feel for who did what at my new job.

I was incredibly happy to find out that my old friend David Geddes from Vancouver had been hired as the director of photography for the show. Just having David there gave me extra confidence and also gave me the inside scoop on what was happening with the show from a "below the line" perspective.

I discovered that our show was to be a nonunion show, as FOX was not a "network." After talking with Dave and several of the crew about the situation, I went into the front office to meet our producer.

For whatever reason, this guy started lying right to my face. I couldn't believe it.

I walked out of his office and called Aaron Spelling. Aaron took my call, and I said, "Mr. Spelling, I don't know who this guy is who you have as our producer here on the stages, but you need to get rid of him." I was furious but kept my tone calm.

Aaron thanked me for calling, and when I showed up twenty-four hours later for the first day of work, the man had vanished.

I had ambitions far beyond acting; someday I wanted to direct as well. I knew that in Aaron I could have a mentor with an absolute wealth of wisdom about the business. I meant to show him that I was ready for any challenge. He surprised me one day by showing up on set with a football jersey that said QUARTERBACK on it. "You're my quarterback, Jay. Every show needs one. You keep this show together—you're my MVP here."

I took the responsibility and his faith in me very seriously.

Jason and Justine
Priestley
ACTORS / MODELS

My sister's and my comp card from 1975. Everyone has to start somewhere.

Holly Robinson getting ready to go out in 1987. Holly was beautiful, smart, and sophisticated, and I still wonder why she was with me for the short time she was.

Holly and me on the inter-island flight in Tahiti. How fat is my face?

Robyn Lively and I met on the set of the film *Teen Angel Returns* in Phoenix, Arizona. I fell for her hard and fast. Thankfully she felt the same way.

With Robyn Lively in 1989. Man, I loved that girl and she loved me. Robyn was truly special and I should have been better to her.

Robyn and me at a party in Vancouver circa December 1989. How can I tell? One word: *Kokanee!*

When you break up with someone, you break up with their whole family. Here I am with my second favorite Lively girl, an adorable two-year-old Blake.

With Shannen and Jamie Kellner outside the FOX jet on our way to that first "upfronts." Our show was such a last-minute pickup, there were no more commercial flights.

Luke took this photo of me on the train ride from Zurich to Zermatt. We took a lot of photos. It helped us pass the time on the four-hour trip.

The three amigos in front of the Matterhorn. This was the last trip we took where we still had our anonymity. Our lives were about to change forever.

Ian and me with the doll we used during the "Two Men and a Baby" episode. Look at Ian's sweater.

One of the Polaroids from that first-season gallery shoot. Luke and I never took anything too seriously.

Steve Young guested on our show and played football with us in the Walshes' front yard. This was one of the moments when I realized our show had become part of pop culture.

Jennie, Shannen, and me with Darren Star at dinner in NYC. Life is good when you're on a hit TV show!

The cast flipping the bird. We had a lot of fun together.

John Hurt taught me invaluable things about acting and life.

Aaron didn't come to the set often. When he did it was a big deal.
This is from June 1991, that first year at the Beach Club. We took a
big risk that season shooting summer episodes, but it really paid off.

I was incredibly fortunate to have Burt Reynolds appear in the first episode of television I ever directed, "She Came in Through the Bathroom Window," in 1993.

Bernie loved party tricks. . . . This one's not so impressive. . . .

Runaround Sue eventually had enough and Brad bought a
Jeep Cherokee (all the rage back then). I took this photo of
him driving it right after he bought it.

Christine and me in Antigua. Judging by the size of my high tops, I'm going to say circa 1995.

"I choose me!" was a line from the show that led to endless hours of comedy between me, Jennie, and Luke.

The girls hanging out—Tori Spelling, Jennie Garth, and Lisa Ragland, Ian's girlfriend at the time, with photographer Paul Robinson.

Me in a pensive mood in a Polacolor photo, before there were selfies.

Swifty loved cheese . . . he was French! Here he is eyeing
an entire wheel of brie. A moment after I took this picture,
he stole that entire wheel of cheese.

My best bud going for a ride.

I always have fun at photo shoots. And that usually means putting on the craziest thing I can find. For this shot I grabbed a women's overcoat that looked ridiculous. Everyone had a good laugh. And, of course, that's the shot they used.

Chasen's
West Hollywood
90048

We were young, we were beautiful, we lived in glamorous locales and lived dramatic teenage lives—but nobody was watching us. The ratings were so-so, and the reviews were absolutely brutal. Every single TV reviewer in the country, it seemed, felt the need to unload on just how dreadful television programming could be, using our show as their prime example. There were no Kids' Choice Awards back then; at that time it was quite revolutionary to aim a show at high schoolers. Teenagers and young adults still watched the same shows as their parents, often with their parents. *90210* was prime time for young people, focusing on issues young people cared about, in a very glamorous setting. Man, how the reviewers hated it. They *hated* it: the scripts, the writing, and the acting. They were particularly cruel to a bunch of young actors.

I kept my eye on the prize: the work, the work, the work. If what we as actors and producers and writers were doing on that soundstage was no good, there would be no fans. The better we could make the show, the more fans we would win and the more adulation we would get. Hopefully, we would even gain a little respect along the way. It was an uphill battle, believe me. Adult viewers hated our show. As the number one guy on the call sheet I felt the pressure. I carried the weight of all those reviewers who demolished us and said our acting was shitty. I took pride in my profession, and I was going to do my best to prove all of them wrong.

The bond I had established with Aaron continued to grow. Our relationship and the show were still new as the year came to a close and the holiday season rolled around. Probably only five or six episodes of *90210* had aired when I received an invitation to the Spelling Entertainment Christmas party.

Aaron, ironically, was Jewish, but he loved Christmas more than anybody I have ever known. He was simply fascinated by all things Christmas. There were no limits to what he would do to celebrate. This was the man who hauled snow to Bel Air so that his kids, Tori and Randy, could have real snow in their yards when they were children. There were a hundred stories like this, all well chronicled in the press, all true.

His annual Christmas party for Spelling Entertainment employees during the first year of *90210* was held in the back room of the show business hangout called Chasen's. Aaron hadn't had a show on the air for a couple of years, so he had a small staff. Before we came along it was generally assumed Aaron was finished; he would ride off into the sunset with his money.

The party was a fun, intimate affair. There was one little food table, with a beautiful turkey on display, and two tables for ten, which was enough seating for his entire staff plus invited guests, including Robyn and me.

Eight years later, when I attended my final Spelling Entertainment Christmas party, there would be more than four hundred people packed into the big events room at the Beverly Wilshire Hotel.

La Jolla Avenue
West Hollywood
90069

I could not even begin to estimate how many different people had passed through that house on La Jolla over the years; Brad was the mainstay. Once he got his own place, he refused to leave. He lived there for years while everyone came and went around him. The place itself was your basic two-bedroom duplex furnished in late '80s frat house. There was frequently a third roommate for varying amounts of time who crashed on the sofa, and guests who might stay for a night or two weeks. Brad had a number of girlfriends who came and went . . . a supersweet girl named Jill, then actress Juliette Lewis.

When Bernie eventually left, Top Forty Gordie moved in. Gordie was a former male stripper from Vancouver whom I'd known forever. We'd been on a *21 Jump Street* episode together. He, along with Bernie and me, Paul Johansson, and Bruce Corkham, were the Canadian contingent of our group. Then there was Dave Sherrill, of course, and Bill "Bring-me-down-ziger" Danziger, a young agent at a small agency called Triad who represented Brad and Bernie. This was our core group of guys.

You can understand how I, standing next to Brad and Paul, a male stripper, was never the "good-looking one." I was always thought of as a pretty-good-looking guy back home, but as soon as I got to L.A.

and started hanging out with this crew, I was just another guy, and not special at all. Time to work on my craft . . .

A couple of weeks after Aaron's party, after the actual Christmas holiday, a bunch of us gathered at Brad's house for an informal holiday gift exchange. Brad had returned from his hometown of Springfield, Missouri, where he had spent Christmas Day with his family. All the regulars showed up ready to party. There was a lot to celebrate. Brad had recently wrapped his role in the highly anticipated film *Thelma and Louise*. It was a huge break, and we were all sincerely happy for him. For a group of actors, there was very little jealousy. We all wanted good roles, but if we didn't get them, we wanted our buddies to get them, not some stranger.

All the guys started arriving, each lugging in a cardboard box containing gifts. Brad took some good-natured ribbing over his supposedly secret relationship with Geena Davis. Ever since he'd returned from location, he was always sneaking off to see her. He went to her place, of course: she was a major movie star, recently split from Jeff Goldblum, who wouldn't have come near that duplex. Brad tried to keep it all quiet and on the down-low, but he had made the mistake of confiding in Bernie one night—which meant that we all instantly knew everything there was to know.

What a surprise: every single guy there gave every other guy a bottle of booze. Oh yeah, somebody gave everyone a carton of cigarettes. Except for our host. Brad had returned from Missouri with a box of Bibles. There was one for each of us, with our names embossed in gold on the faux-leather cover next to a tiny cross. He was handing out personalized Bibles while his cardboard box filled up with gifts of liquor bottles topped by a carton of cigs.

If you could have seen the looks on our faces. I mean everyone's faces! Brad was so pleased with himself he could not stop smiling. All the rest of the twentysomething actor guys were—for once—actually speechless. The whole crew had been laughing, joking, passing around holiday-edition bottles of Jack Daniel's and firing up Marlboro Lights . . . and then our host presented each of us with a Bible and stopped the party cold. For a second, anyway. It was quite a moment.

Six months later a firestorm would erupt when *Thelma and Louise* opened in every theater in the United States. Brad was on the brink of ten-million-dollar paychecks and film sets all over the world. My struggling show on a fledgling network would soon be beamed into ten million homes all over the world every week. And Bernie? He would become infamous—in our group at least—but for slightly different reasons. There are ten million *stories* I could tell about Bernie.

My Bible still sits on a bookshelf in my library. Every now and then a guest will see my name on the cover, pick it up off the shelf, and look at it quizzically, knowing I'm not a big churchgoer. They usually say something like, "I didn't know you were a Bible reader." I smile and tell them it was a gift from an old friend.

Beverly Hills 90210

It simply amazes me that twenty years later anyone would possibly care, but judging from the questions I get, plenty of people still want to know: during the shooting of *90210,* did everyone hook up with everyone else in real life? The answer to that is simple. We were a bunch of young, attractive people in our early twenties who were thrown together for ten, twelve, fourteen hours a day. What do you think happened? Of course various combinations of people slept with each other over the years. If you were in that situation, trust me, you would have done it, too.

But the main thing to remember is this: in the grand scheme of things, all these hookups were very minor flings. Every single cast member working on that show was much too smart to let an "office romance" and what might happen one night after work impact what we did on the set. Our jobs and the show were much more important to all of us. Plus, we all saw enough of each other at work; we were constantly together. There were plenty of guest stars for distraction, as well as regular boyfriends and girlfriends. I was very caught up in my romance with Robyn; any limited spare time I had, I wanted to spend with her.

Shannen particularly had a complicated love life. For a while she was dating some real estate guy in Chicago, flying back and forth all the time. She eventually left him for his closest friend, another Chicago guy. None of this was surprising; Shannen was a very impulsive girl. She always seemed to be between houses or places to live. With three main girls on the show—Shannen, Jennie, and Tori—and their various boyfriends coming and going, there was always some drama going on. The guys—Luke, Ian, Young Bri, and I—did our best to stay out of it. We had an easier time hanging out together. Our end of the hallway was much calmer.

Toward the end of an official FOX event one night, Luke and I were getting ready to take off when Aaron came over to speak to us. It had been some sort of promotional party, with plenty of alcohol flowing. Aaron was in a happy, expansive mood. "Jason. Luke," he said in that gruff voice. "You guys need to come back to my house! You've got to see it!"

The final touches had just been completed on Spelling Manor, and he could not wait to show it off. He was like a little kid with a new toy—absolutely delighted. The three of us had been doing some drinking that night . . . we were all half in the bag as we pretty much stumbled out of the back of his limousine and into Spelling Manor.

"Look, look, the Renoir," he pointed out immediately as we opened the massive wooden front door and walked into the cavernous entrance hall. A tiny original Renoir painting hung on the wall in plain sight, within arm's reach.

"Holy crap, Aaron, somebody's going to pocket that one day on the way out!" I said.

"No, no . . ." He waved his hands around vaguely. "There's security, Jason, and cameras all over the place," he said as we took in our surroundings. Luke and I were literally in shock as the house tour proceeded. Our reaction to the sheer immensity and opulence of the Manor could be accurately described as What. The. Fuck!

Aaron was particularly anxious to take us to the basement. We made a quick stop in a room downstairs with wall-to-wall glass cases holding a vast array of hundreds of dolls of every imaginable size, shape, and costume. "Candy's doll collection," he said. Of course there was a private bar in the basement level, where we stopped to have another drink. There was an extensive alcohol selection; more brands were available than at most high-end hotel bars, including draft beer. "Dude! He's got a tap in his house, unbelievable!" With all the wonders surrounding us, Luke and I thought that was the coolest thing ever.

We all grabbed a beer—none of us needed another—and proceeded to the pièce de résistance: the bowling alley. Aaron snapped on the lights, and a full-size two-lane bowling alley came to life. He pushed a couple more buttons, and the official scoreboard lit up, the pins reset, and bowling balls popped up in the machine. Unable to contain himself, Aaron proceeded to kick off his shoes and head in his stocking feet over to the lanes. He grabbed a bowling ball, ran up to the line, heaved the ball down the lane, and slipped on the highly polished wood floor and landed in a heap, groaning.

Luke and I were flipping out. Our first year on a new job with Aaron! Had our elderly, slightly frail boss just broken his hip in a freak bowling alley accident with the two of us just standing by? We ran over and picked him up and anxiously set him on his feet again.

"Aaron, Aaron, are you all right?" Thankfully, he was fine. Nothing was broken; he was just a bit shaken up. Though not nearly as shaken up as the two of us. We wanted out, pronto. "So that was supercool, Aaron; this was an amazing tour. Maybe it's time for you to go to bed now. We better take off . . . it's late . . ." We were backpedaling like crazy. We wanted our boss safe in bed and ourselves off the premises. We got the hell out of there. That little tour/party ended rather abruptly.

Aaron was such a good guy; he retold that story fifty times, cracking up every single time. How he loved that house. That quality of childlike enthusiasm and the sheer delight he took in the things he loved was a wonderfully endearing trait.

Spago
West Hollywood
90069

Our first season, there just weren't that many people watching the show. I could go anywhere and do anything completely unrecognized and unbothered. I don't think one person approached me the entire first year *90210* was on the air. I certainly wasn't famous, although L.A. was not the best barometer as people tend to be fairly jaded about actors and leave them in peace.

Back then, a standard television order was pilot plus twelve episodes, for a total of thirteen—half a season, to see how well the show does. Cast and crew are then waiting on pins and needles to see if the network would order another nine episodes—a back-nine pickup order—to make it a full twenty-two-episode season. At the last minute, *90210* got a back-nine pickup order for its first season.

In the early months of 1991, the Gulf War was drawing to a close, and all the TV stations at the time—NBC, CBS, ABC, and CNN—showed round-the-clock nonstop coverage. Operation Desert Storm was the first "televised war," and for a while the whole country, it seemed, tuned in. It was huge. FOX was the only network that continued to broadcast regular entertainment programming most of the time.

As the war wound down we saw our numbers slowly, slowly start to climb as the viewing audience got sick and tired of watching war coverage. People were now looking for the opposite of reality. They wanted to be distracted and entertained. FOX was there; and it was pretty much the only network airing entertainment.

Barry Diller had the brilliant idea of having *90210* return to the air early the following season. We started shooting new shows at the end of May so FOX would have new original programming to air starting in the middle of July. That was quite a bold move at the time; he was looking to capture the teen audience who had nothing else to do in the summertime. With the right show, they would watch TV—we often forget that back then, there was no Internet or cell phones, and watching movies meant going to the theater or going to a video store to rent videotapes to put in a VCR. There was a huge untapped market of teenagers out there looking for entertainment, for sure.

So we started filming the summertime-themed shows: Brandon started working at the Beverly Hills Beach Club . . . Dylan got into a surfing accident . . . stuff like that, and it worked. That summer the show really began to take off. The first episode of season two premiered at number 14, which was a very big deal for FOX at that time. It resulted in an invitation for Shannen, Luke, and me to present at the Emmy Awards. Our own show was never nominated for an Emmy, but I was a presenter three times.

I was still new to the game; my change in status was so sudden and surprising that when my new publicist, Eddie, asked me, "You've been invited to the after-party at Spago—want to go?" my response was "What Spago party?"

"Jason, you know what that is. Everybody goes there!" I had heard of the restaurant on Sunset, but I was not at all clued in to any after-parties anywhere. I made a brief, unmemorable stop there, because I thought I should, but I was just so unhip to the whole scene. I didn't know who Wolfgang Puck was. I had no idea about Spago's famous pizza. I was a very naive kid who worked all the time. Luke and I drank in craphole Valley restaurant/bars like Marix Tex Mex and Casa Vega after work some nights, surrounded by forty-year-olds who had no idea who we were and would not have cared one bit if they had known.

Still, my life was suddenly moving and changing and picking up momentum rapidly. It was both exciting and unsettling. I began to feel a bit under the gun. I was twenty-two years old; I had no idea how to balance a full-time career on a successful show with a romantic relationship. It seemed to me, at the time, that what I needed was to be as commitment-free as possible so I could be nimble and agile when necessary. The breakup with Robyn crushed me, even though I initiated it. To her credit, Robyn seemed to understand what I was going through. She knew it was best to let me go off to deal with this whole new life that was barreling my way. We parted as a couple, though she remains a friend to this day. But it was a very, very long time before I stopped torturing myself with bittersweet what-ifs.

For years I grieved over the loss of this relationship and wondered if I had made a mistake. Though everything certainly turned out fine in the end—we are both happily married to great spouses with beautiful kids—we were still not much more than kids ourselves back then. So when I look back, I can forgive myself for what happened.

The High Desert
Kern County
93263

The first half of the second season of the show was a perfect balance: the show was successful and gaining fans and momentum every week, but there was no hysteria surrounding us. It was clear we were on the right path, an enviable situation for cast and crew alike as we all really settled into our jobs. Kevin Caffrey was best boy electric on *90210*. I walked into his office one day and saw a bunch of racing posters on the walls. "Dude, I've always wanted to race rally cars," I told him. "Is there a rally series here in Southern California?"

"I'm sure there is, let me find out." Kevin looked into it and found out that there were all kinds of races in the area, sponsored by the California Rally Series.

Rally races are car races on rough dirt roads driven by teams of two. Each car leaves the starting point at one- or two-minute intervals. The various "stages" of the course are connected with "transits" on public roads, where the cars must obey the posted speed limits and rules of the road. The courses go hundreds of miles in two-day rallies. The team with the best combined times from every competition stage wins. It's a very popular sport worldwide; I had been following it since I was a kid.

I finally had enough money to buy a rally car and start competing. Kevin and I started looking for the right car. Eventually, we settled on a Honda CRX that we bought for about three thousand bucks and tinkered with endlessly. We "campaigned" that car for a year. That's not a political term; in performance rallying, "campaign" simply means to race. Performance rally races were held on weekends, day and night, on the distant outskirts of Los Angeles, way down dirt roads you'd never seen before and had no idea were even out there. The roads were so remote and primitive they were maintained by the Forest Service, and barreling through those ridges late at night could most definitely be dangerous.

Kevin and I would haul our car to the track in a trailer, unload it, prepare it, jump in, and race as fast as we could. I drove while he navigated. Our Honda was cheap and slow, but we raced the crap out of that car all over California for an entire year. Ridgecrest, Glen Helen, Gorman, Santa Rosa, the high desert. This was grassroots, mom-and-pop racing. Rally racing is the most fun you can have with your clothes on!

One weekend I was going out of town to promote the show and told KC he should take a turn as driver. "You drive it this weekend, buddy," I urged him. I left, and of course he immediately drove our car off a cliff and wadded it up. We had to literally cut the car in half and scrap the wrecked half. We searched all over California for another wrecked CRX so we could basically weld the two halves together and have a car again.

The two of us were just having fun together, competing in these races for a good time. It was very much a hobby, and not an extremely hazardous one. Our car just didn't go fast enough; it maxed out at approximately 135 miles per hour and had a full roll cage, race seats, and seven-point harnesses. Of course, we also wore full-on racing suits and helmets. Somehow, somewhere along the way we started winning our class, and eventually even won some rallies. Next thing we knew, Toyota called and said, "How would you like to race for us next year? We'll set you up with a Celica GT4. We'll build it out for you, and you go campaign that next year."

"Yeah, sure. Okay!" We both jumped on this offer. KC and I had become very close; we worked long hours on the show together during the week and raced together most weekends. None of my cast mates were particularly interested in racing, and I was careful not to talk much about it at work. That was the whole point, to me, of racing: to take me away. Driving leaves you no room to worry about anything else. It concentrates mind and body in a way that nothing else I had ever tried did. Racing was all-consuming; it required every bit of my focus and attention. There was no room to think about the show when I was in a race.

I loved being on *90210,* but the hours were long and the pressure on me was intense. Just like everybody else with a stressful job, I needed an outlet. I loved racing cars because, to me, it was so pure. A race is a race. There's only one winner. It was straight-up competition all the way to a finish line, down to a stopwatch and winning or losing by hundredths of a second. There was a clarity to racing that I couldn't find anywhere else in my life, and I cherished it.

Torrance
90501

Ironically, *Beverly Hills 90210,* a show featuring the lives of kids in one of the country's richest, most exclusive neighborhoods, was actually shot in the most unglamorous places imaginable. Mainly we filmed at a studio in Van Nuys, a suburb of the Valley known for being the porn capital of the world. Sherman Oaks, Altadena, Pasadena, Glendale, Eagle Rock—we shot everywhere *but* Beverly Hills!

FOX producers had approached the real Beverly Hills High School for permission to film the show on their campus before the pilot and were turned down. So Torrance High School—another suburb out by Los Angeles International Airport—stood in for West Beverly High. During the first season and the beginning of the second season, our presence was no big deal to anyone there. We were just some random television show that showed up now and then to shoot some scenes.

Los Angeles residents are accustomed to filming, so no one really paid much attention to us. But, as the show blew up, we started spending more time shooting at Torrance High School. By this time the students there most definitely knew who we were, and they all loved the show. Well, let me clarify that statement. Girls loved the show; guys did not.

Our production company had only one assistant director and a trainee AD managing the whole set, so keeping people away from us while we were working wasn't a big priority. In all fairness, it wasn't exactly a problem at first. It was one thing to have giggling high school girls coming over and asking for autographs and pictures and stuff. It was another when the senior-year boys started hurling insults and doing their best to start shit with Ian, Brian, Luke, and me. There were quite a few girls with crushes and quite a few pissed-off, jealous boyfriends.

One day Brian and I were in the middle of a scene when some hulking football player–type guys mouthed off nonstop as we tried to work. They were showing off for their friends, calling the actors names. I was a few years older than these guys, while at eighteen Brian was exactly their age, though neither of us came close to their size and bulk. One guy in particular would not shut up until he got a rise out of one of us. He went way past acceptable words and behavior, and I finally took the bait.

I turned around and started walking toward him. "I don't care how old you are, kid. You say that to me one more time and I'm going to put you in the hospital." He started coming toward me; I grabbed his shirt, he grabbed mine, everyone on the crew jumped in to stop what was about to happen and what do you know . . . the next day we had security guards. Lots of them, all around us, all the time, from that point on. But it took a near brawl in the hallway. Nobody had even thought about security before. The rapidly increasing success of the show had caught everybody by surprise. Nobody had any idea of what we were dealing with back then; we were all in uncharted waters.

The show had its own publicist, and there were numerous FOX and Spelling publicists all over the place, but I felt that I needed someone who was minding my personal agenda. I wanted to capitalize on the increasing success of the show, of course, but I was already wary of getting typecast as Brandon. I made sure I had someone working primarily to keep me established as Jason Priestley, actor, not Brandon, though I would never get completely away from questions about the show. Eddie Michaels, my publicist, was young, just a few years older than me, but smart and aggressive and wouldn't take no for an answer.

It was a big, big deal when I was asked to appear on the *Late Night with David Letterman* show in November of 1991. Back then, teens weren't a big market. Someone like Dave had no interest in a "kid's show." Adults didn't watch the show, so why would teens? David Letterman was an idol even then, especially among college students, who watched his show religiously. The man was a comedy icon and could be legendarily mean to guests he didn't like. He could get quite testy, so I was sweating backstage as I waited to be called to join him.

"Coming out next is young actor Jason Priestley. He's on this new show, *Beverly Hills 90210,* which is about . . . hmmm . . . it's about these rich kids . . . and they . . . What do they do? What exactly do these kids do?" he turned to Paul Shaffer.

I yelled from behind the curtain, "They have problems, Dave, lots of problems!" He cracked up.

"I see, I see, rich kids in Beverly Hills. I am sure they *do* have lots of problems. Bring Jason out here!"

Once I got onstage and sat down I felt much better. My fellow Canadian Paul made me feel relaxed, and Dave had already laughed, so I was in good shape. It was a fun visit.

Less than a month later, I was on the *Tonight Show* with Jay Leno.

Amsterdam
1017 BV

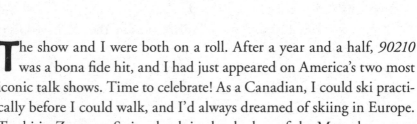

The show and I were both on a roll. After a year and a half, *90210* was a bona fide hit, and I had just appeared on America's two most iconic talk shows. Time to celebrate! As a Canadian, I could ski practically before I could walk, and I'd always dreamed of skiing in Europe. To ski in Zermatt, Switzerland, in the shadow of the Matterhorn, was any skier's dream. Luke and Ian joined me during the holiday winter break, and we took off with plans to meet up with a couple more of our friends in Amsterdam for New Year's Eve.

The village of Zermatt is a perfect little Swiss storybook village. No cars are allowed, and everything is pulled by horse and sleigh . . . it's like walking into a fairy-tale illustration.

The show was not on the air in Switzerland, so the German-speaking natives couldn't have cared less who we were, but there were a few tourists in town making a fuss over us. Our rowdy behavior soon led all the staffers in our hotel and the local bars to call us the "crazy TV Americans." Ian hooked up with a random American girl, so Luke and I gave him a hard time. "Had to come to Switzerland to find an American chick? Couldn't manage that back home?"

One night at the Grand Hotel Zermatterhof, we were walking through the grand old building, winding our way through lots of narrow little corridors and hallways. Literally every time we turned a corner it seemed, somebody plowed into Luke and knocked him down. There had already been plenty of beverages consumed at happy hour, so we might have been a little shaky to start. Still, we seemed to be directly in the path of every huge Austrian dude in town, all hurrying through the hotel, literally knocking him down on his ass and not even looking back. I was in the right place, somehow, and managed to stay out of their way. Finally, some old guy who was at least seventy years old came charging around the corner, and *boom!*, he knocked Luke over just as we were nearing the main entrance. My friend jumped up in the middle of the lobby with his fists up.

"Okay, listen up! One more old Austrian motherfucker knocks me down, we're gonna go!" he shouted. It was hilarious. I could not stop laughing. All hundred thirty pounds of him . . . ready to take on the whole country. . . . Instead, we just went to the bar and had another drink.

The concierge at the hotel told me about the availability of a private helicopter that flew from Zermatt to Geneva, where we then planned to catch a flight to Amsterdam to ring in New Year's Eve 1992. The show was a hit, we were all assured a job . . . so we were all suddenly blasé enough to say, sure, let's take chopper through the Alps at about $1,000 per passenger. Quite a change in status for a guy who hadn't had a television or full tank of gas only two short years earlier.

The quaint cobblestone lanes of Amsterdam are never easy to navigate, but on New Year's Eve, smack in the middle of the red-light district, it was so crowded we could barely move. Every single resident and all the tourists were out; every street was packed with people.

We took in the scene with wide eyes—it was hard to tell if this was a party or a war zone. Guys launched bottle rockets across the canals while others set off far too many exploding fireworks. I saw guys literally shoving quarter sticks of dynamite into empty Heineken bottles and throwing them into random groups of people. Everyone was behaving in a shockingly reckless and dangerous manner. It goes without saying that everyone was drunk and stoned, of course; that's just part of the Amsterdam experience. It was utter mad mayhem and an absolutely perfect scene for a bunch of young guys. We loved it!

As midnight approached, I got separated from Ian and Luke at some point and wound up standing by myself on a small bridge over a canal at midnight. I turned my face to the sky as it literally rained fire for minutes on end, the noise from the explosions rising to a deafening pitch as confetti and ashes blew all around me. I savored a moment of absolute, perfect happiness. I'd just skied the Alps for a week. I had reached my goal of becoming a successful working actor. Fame so far had been mostly fun, not terribly invasive. I had two good friends accompanying me—on two journeys: *90210* and this amazing trip. This vacation marked the last time any one of the three of us would travel around Europe—or anywhere else, pretty much—anonymously. It was our last hurrah.

Smashbox Studio
Westwood
90024

Back in those more innocent days, mall appearances used to be commonplace for young performers. That's how many teen acts, in the music business especially, used to get their start. All of us cast members had made a series of trips to various megamalls across the country to promote the show in its first year. These personal appearances were effective: the crowds grew steadily bigger, and in the second year the show really caught fire. On one occasion, Luke, Shannen, and Jennie were completely taken by surprise when thousands of kids showed up to see them at a mall—they had expected a couple hundred at best. There was a near riot, and my friends were sneaked out of the building in a laundry cart.

My own publicity roll continued in the New Year . . . every time I turned around, I was talking to a reporter from *Bop* or *Teen Beat* or any one of the many, many magazines catering to young readers. In every single interview from that time, I'm smoking cigarettes and drinking in a bar . . . something every journalist made note of. Looking back, it's a little bit shocking to see so many of these incidents, all in print. Clearly, I had a bit of a chip on my shoulder. I was out to prove that I was nothing like the sanctimonious Brandon Walsh. I was going to show them. . . . Come with me . . . we're gonna get drunk and tear up the town! I'm Jason Priestley, not Brandon!

Perhaps this is why I got the tabloid reputation I did. There were all kinds of lurid stories about me being out of control . . . boozing it up in Hollywood . . . that Christian Slater took me to an AA meeting. "Jason's let success go to his head and he's been drinking like he's immortal," a nameless source said. "He likes to go to bars that are dark and smoky." Did I like dark and smoky bars? Sure, why not! But the rest of this kind of stuff was so ridiculous and false . . . I'd never met Christian Slater, I didn't go to a meeting, and I wasn't any more out of control than any other twenty-two-year-old guy.

I did, however, do myself plenty of harm with my own antics when doing press. Drinking hard during interviews probably wasn't a good idea, but, again, I wanted everyone to see I was *not* Brandon. "Jason likes to have a good time, but he doesn't have a drinking problem," the reliable Eddie said. It was true.

Rolling Stone scheduled a cover shoot for Luke, Shannen, and me in Los Angeles, to take place on a weekend because we were shooting all week long. I went out somewhere the Friday night before the shoot and wound up staying out very late. When I woke up the next morning I most definitely did not feel like going to a cover shoot—nor did I look like a cover boy! Fortunately, like every twenty-two-year-old, I had the ability to go out and get wild, stay out late, grab a few hours' sleep, then get up the next day and do what I had to do . . . looking fine. That's the great part of being twenty-two . . . for everyone!

Andrew Eccles, the famous celebrity photographer, met the three of us at a huge rented studio over in West L.A. on Pico Boulevard. He had all kinds of creative ideas. We played around with a bunch of concepts, like one of us pushing the others in a laundry cart in a nod to the recent riot, and all kinds of other stuff. In the end he went with a more traditional shot. It was a huge honor to be on the cover of *Rolling Stone*—that year we were in the company of other cover subjects including Bono, President Clinton, Michael Jackson, Tom Cruise, Nirvana, and Bruce Springsteen. I didn't have time to fully slow down and appreciate what a big deal it really was. It was immediately back to work and then on to the next big event.

The Golden Globe Awards, where film and television stars mingle together, really is one big long party, just as it appears on television. It's a full-on banquet, the fancy version of a rubber chicken dinner, and its reputation as a place where the stars get smashed is well earned. The bar is wide open, and by the time the last awards are presented, everyone in attendance has been sitting there for literally hours getting tanked.

In January of 1992, Luke and I were asked to present an award. The idea was to have the two teen idols from the hot new show nominated for Best Drama present an award. *Beverly Hills 90210* had caught on like wildfire in Europe, and the Globes, of course, were sponsored by the Hollywood Foreign Press Association.

Luke and I lived in different parts of town, so we arrived at the Golden Globes separately. I got dressed to the nines and was picked up in a limousine, walked the red carpet, and was interviewed and photographed by the international press. Back in those days, no fans showed up, just the press.

The show was running on Thursday nights at this time, up against *Cheers* and the popular block of NBC shows that had dominated the ratings for years. Apparently, we were giving the longtime favorite a run for its money. Luke and I got up from our table as the time to present drew near. We headed for the men's room before going backstage. Just as we were walking in, the door opened and there was Ted Danson walking out. He stopped and pointed very sternly at both of us. "You two. Knock it off! Just stop!" he said and walked away.

Luke and I were floored. "Dude, that was Ted Danson!" we kept saying to each other. That encounter was much more exciting than going onstage as presenters. I also got to meet Jodie Foster that night, who had just won for *Silence of the Lambs*. This was another real thrill for me, so much so that by the end of the night, it didn't even matter that we didn't win. It was such an unforgettable experience just to be there.

Studio 8H
New York
10112

It was a truly golden time in the storied history of one of the greatest television series ever. No, not *90210*—*Saturday Night Live*! In addition to my fellow Canadians Mike Myers and Phil Hartman, there was Chris Rock, David Spade, Chris Farley, Adam Sandler, Rob Schneider, Al Franken, Victoria Jackson, and Julia Sweeney in the cast. Just a few weeks after presenting at the Globes, my show's producers gave me a week off to host *SNL*, the experience of a lifetime.

I made one quick stop in New York first, calling on publisher Jann Wenner at his office to see our cover of *Rolling Stone*. Jann had all kinds of motorcycle memorabilia around, and as I was very much into bikes, I mentioned that I rode. He lit up on that topic, very curious, asking me what kind of bike I had (Yamaha FZR600) and where I rode (all over). We planned a ride soon . . . that over the years turned into many. It was always great to find a true kindred spirit in the adventure-seeking department!

It didn't get more exciting that hosting a live comedy show. My week started bright and early on Monday morning in a conference room in the 30 Rock building. First thing all the writers gathered around with a stack of their new work. Each cast member took a turn presenting his or her material—some was new, some was stuff they'd been working on for a while. All of them were constantly working on bits, sometimes for months.

Everyone knew in advance that I was the guest host that week, so they came prepared. I read a bunch of stuff cold; I was really thrown into it: they just hand you a stack of script pages and you start working on bits right there at the table with no chance to prepare. It's challenging, and I could see that it could be quite intimidating, but my early acting lessons had included improv and I loved it. Lorne Michaels ran the whole meeting; I had never met him before and found his way of working beyond inspiring.

We split up, and all the writers then polished their best bits for a day or so, then on Tuesday we all met again. Same process: I read more bits and then we started staging and getting acts up on their feet. Certain sketches started falling by the wayside, and slowly a comedy show emerged. The pace was incredibly fast; by Friday night dress rehearsal the show was in a pretty good place. Lorne made a few last cuts on Saturday after the final dress rehearsal . . . and there it was, the show I was going to host. Live.

Because the 1992 Winter Olympics were happening in France, Phil Hartman, Dana Carvey, and I did a sketch where I played a figure skater who attempted to medal in the Olympics and gave the worst performance of his career . . . falling over and over again. I shot that bit in a place called SkyRink one day . . . a private rink on the roof of a building in Manhattan. I thought that an enclosed rink on top of a skyscraper was a very cool thing.

I was so challenged and busy and engaged all week that I seriously did not have time get nervous. The week literally flew by. Suddenly there I was, doing my opening monologue. My show flew by so fast, I wished I could do it all over again. I was truly only half joking when I asked Lorne to call my show, get me out of work, and let me stay right there.

Back at my regular job, the producers brought in a new character on *90210* named Emily Valentine. The character was an edgy girl played by a young actress named Christine Elise. She wore jeans and engineer boots and had short, spiky blond hair—a much more alternative look

than any of the other girls on the show. Apart from being beautiful, Christine had a strong, confident energy about her that drew me
toward her. Her very first day on set, she had to pull out a guitar in the
middle of the quad at Torrance High and start singing the Janis Joplin
song . . . "Oh Lord, won't you buy me a Mercedes Benz?"

It was a demanding scene for her first day and she seemed to be
terrified. She went from being this brassy little chick who cursed like
a truck driver and radiated attitude to a nervous wreck when it came
time to sing. I was fascinated by those opposing sides to her personal-
ity: in one moment she could be so confident, so full of herself, so full
of bravado; then the next moment, so stricken with nerves that she was
barely able to pull herself together.

Her scene came out fine, of course . . . once the camera came on,
you would never have known she was even nervous. The dichotomy
intrigued me. I wanted to get to know this girl better. It turned out
that she, like me, had moved to L.A. alone at a young age to pursue her
acting dream. Her family lived far away, in Boston, so that was a strong
bond we shared. We spent more and more time together after that first
day, getting to know each other and quickly became close work friends.

I was still somewhat of a wide-eyed optimist back then; it was just
my nature to always hope for the best in people and expect a happy
outcome in every situation. Christine was far more of a realist. She had
a much more cynical and jaded outlook about work, relationships . . .
everything. I needed a dose of that in my life; I found her perspective
refreshing.

We were shooting more than thirty shows a year, which was fine with
me because I loved my job, but it was a day in, day out grind. I worked
all the time. When I wasn't shooting the show, I was reading scripts,
trying to land roles that might showcase another side of me. I wanted
desperately to get out of the Brandon Walsh box I was clearly already in.

In the past six months I had appeared on *Late Night with David
Letterman*, been on the cover of *Rolling Stone*, and hosted *SNL*. I'd
done tons of print interviews. I'd been a presenter at the Golden
Globes. I had hired a helicopter to fly through the Swiss Alps! I was no
longer living in the real world. I was in Beverly Hills 90210.

St. Helena
Napa Valley
94574

Look, we can't all be George Clooney. I discovered early on that I felt better with a steady girlfriend in my life, a woman of substance as opposed to arm candy. When I was out on the town dating all kinds of women, I didn't love it. I felt a little bit at loose ends, a little lost. Most of my friends had no desire to settle down. Not for years and years, anyway, especially at our age. But I felt lucky that I'd made such an important discovery about myself so soon: that being half of a couple was important to me. I partied less and was an all-around better-behaved guy when I had a steady girlfriend, not to mention that I felt happier and more grounded.

Christine was on *Beverly Hills 90210* for nearly the entire second season (and would return in her recurring role in later years as well). Shortly after the season wrapped, our relationship turned romantic. We didn't purposely wait; it just happened that way. Once we hooked up, things moved fast. One Saturday afternoon we were driving around and found ourselves in the Los Feliz Oaks neighborhood. We saw a house with a For Sale sign and got out of the car to take a look. The next-door neighbor happened to come out of her house just then. "They're having an open house tomorrow," she told us. "Come back then so you can go inside."

Christine and I returned the next day, toured the house, loved it, and made an offer that night. It was accepted and that was that. I rented out my condo to the Nelson twins—Matthew and Gunnar, Ricky Nelson's sons. They'd put out an album that was huge a couple of years before called *After the Rain*. They were making a new record and touring. Christine packed up her little house, and we moved in together as soon as escrow closed.

No doubt years of having no family nearby and being completely on my own made me eager to establish a solid home base. Christine and I moved in with high hopes and lots of plans. We started with some serious remodeling. We put in a new kitchen and added a movie theater in the basement where I watched football on weekends, on the rare Sundays I was at home. Always an enthusiastic amateur cook, I began stockpiling cookbooks and trying new dishes. We both loved to entertain; we started a tradition of throwing a formal Christmas party every year, where men were asked to wear tuxedos and women, formal gowns. It was our miniversion of the Spelling Christmas party . . . very mini! Meanwhile, the gossip rags credited Christine with getting me to tone down my boozing ways with her firm grip on me. Supposedly, I liked her tough love. This was just more silliness.

Christine introduced me to the wonderful world of wine. When I was growing up, my parents drank wine at home, but I never had any idea what good wine could be until I met her and started going to wine tastings. We liked to take road trips to Napa Valley to all the various vineyards and attend private tastings and wine launches. Because I was on a hit TV show, the wineries treated me in a way not many other twenty-three-year-olds hanging around tasting rooms would be received. Right from the start I was lucky to be given an incredible education of the winemaking process by the top experts in the field.

There were some phenomenal wines coming out of California in the early 1990s, and I was given an insider's perspective. This was certainly one time my fame came in very handy; it allowed me access to people and places I would never have been introduced to otherwise. I met all kinds of brilliant vintners and was given a fantastic behind-the-scenes view. Wine became my passion . . . even obsession. Collecting wine. Tasting wine. Throwing tasting parties where I could introduce my other wine-loving friends to wines they didn't know. Our new house had a large wine cellar, and I got busy filling it up.

I had recently seen a photo of a French bulldog on the cover of *Architectural Digest* magazine that really captured my attention. Then, one day, Christine and I happened to be at the Beverly Center, a shopping mall in Los Angeles, where there was a pet store. It was 1993, and pet stores were still around. The horror of puppy mills and the like that supply pet stores hadn't yet become public knowledge. There in a cage sat a tiny champagne French bulldog looking miserable. While the other puppies played, he just sat there, staring straight ahead. We knew nothing about French bulldogs, but it didn't take long for us to decide we needed to save that little guy.

I was lucky; my little Swifty was free of health problems. At only twenty-five pounds, he was portable and traveled the world with me. Super mellow, whatever we did was okay with him. He was the perfect set dog—he somehow sensed when the cameras were rolling. He never barked when he shouldn't—when he heard the word "Rolling," he would sit quietly. When he heard "Cut," he would wander around looking for friends, and he found many of them. He was quite popular with cast and crew alike. A very affable little guy.

My relationship with Christine was my first full-fledged adult relationship. She and I lived together, renovated a house together, owned dogs together, traveled the world together: Ireland, Hawaii—you name it, we went there. She was a busy actress in her own right, plus a wonderful girlfriend. Intelligent, articulate, opinionated, very well spoken, and fun—Christine was captivating. We shared our lives for the next five years.

Perris
92571

We were shooting thirty-two episodes of *90210* a year, which was
an extraordinary number, and our hiatus was very short. Three
or four months a year off is standard; eight weeks was the absolute
minimum we were allowed by contract—and believe me, that's what
we got. Eight weeks to the day. I felt this incredible pressure to find a
movie to do in my hiatus between seasons two and three. Where that
pressure was coming from, or if I was imagining it, I don't know. But
my choices were severely limited by my specific time frame. Still, my
agent, Nick, and I worked around it.

I was going to New York to do some publicity for the show, and
Nick gave me three scripts to read on the five-hour flight. "All three
would work, time-wise, with your hiatus, so read them all and give
me a call when you get there," he told me as he handed me the stack.
I read all three on the plane, and the one I liked the best was called
Calendar Girl. The story was set in the '60s, and I would be playing
the lead, a high school kid named Roy Darpinian who was obsessed
with Marilyn Monroe. I liked that it was a buddy picture, about three
friends from a small town going on a wild cross-country road trip/
adventure. How could I not love a story about some brash teenage
guys driving a huge old car to Hollywood in search of their dreams?

I also liked that the movie was a period piece set in the much simpler year of 1962. The underlying theme to the somewhat silly caper

was young guys taking one last, final adventure before their real lives as men began—with all the growing up and compromising and losing their ideals that would entail. Their journey was set in the final golden days of the country's innocence and hopefulness, just before it would become roiled by the loss of the president and involvement in Vietnam. Or perhaps I was reading way too much lofty hidden meaning into a movie script!

When I got back to L.A., I met with Penny Marshall, the producer, and John Whitesell, her director. The three of us discussed the character of Roy and whether or not I was I right for the part. Penny had really come into her own after a successful acting career. She had received tremendous critical acclaim for the Robin Williams picture *Awakenings*. She was a very smart woman, and I also liked her personally. I felt that I would be in good hands with her.

John was in somewhat of a similar position as me; he was a successful television director looking to branch out into movies, just as I was with my acting career. There was a very clear division back then between television and movie projects, with movies being considered by far the more prestigious medium for both actors and directors. These days people jump back and forth . . . in fact, the pendulum has swung to where movie actors are actively seeking TV roles!

The rest of the cast was great: Jerry O'Connell from *Stand by Me* played my main sidekick, along with Joey Pantoliano and a number of other good, solid actors who were on board. The whole project seemed promising; the film seemed like the right match for me. The character of Roy was a boxer in the movie, and the big climactic scene was when Roy actually steps into the ring and fights his father, played by Steve Railsback. Steve did awesome work on that movie; I could not have been more impressed, and the two of us became very close.

However, I had to be in the proper shape to play a boxer. For the first time in my career, I needed a personal trainer. I worked with a guy named Eddie Wilde, who was phenomenal. He was huge, a European bodybuilding champ, and I have to say he supervised a remarkable transformation of my physique in a short amount of time. It was painful; I guess it had to be to be so fast and effective. That man could train! The character of Roy had to be a very ripped little guy, like a real boxer, and Eddie managed to give me a convincing boxer's body.

My training consisted entirely of work with weights. No cardio or anything else . . . just weight training. Eddie and I met every day, six days a week, and I trained with him for about three months. My diet was incredibly restrictive. It was all protein: egg whites and fish, but only certain kinds of fish . . . tuna and shark, mainly. No fat. No carbs except a piece of dry toast each day. Lots of vegetables. No salt, no oil, no butter, no alcohol . . .

If you've ever wondered how actors manage to transform their bodies the way they do, it's because they go on diets like that and follow them to the letter. They do their workout every day, giving 110 percent effort, and follow their trainer's direction exactly. Actors can do it, in short, because they're getting paid to do it and it's their job. Part of being an actor is dedication to your craft, and your craft might include physical transformation to inhabit a character. It's that simple . . . not easy, but simple.

We shot the film in Perris (just outside Los Angeles) and in Los Angeles, California, and wrapped it up in six weeks. Jerry, Gabriel Olds, and I got along fine as the three friends, and I felt that we played off one another quite convincingly. If this was shooting a major motion picture, I was all for it. There was absolutely nothing about the process that I didn't like.

Of course, once the movie wrapped, I had to jump right back into season three of *90210* with barely a breather. For the rest of the year, however, I knew in the back of my mind I had a movie coming. It premiered the following March in a blaze of Columbia Studios publicity. I flew to New York to do a press junket, donated the shoes I wore in the film to Planet Hollywood, the cool place at the time, and did a ton of press. Then the reviews started rolling in. They were not kind. Brutal, in fact. Again . . . just like *90210*.

When the film opened, the returns were not great, and the movie quickly vanished. It was disappointing at the time, of course, but I certainly did not realize the repercussions this one project would have on the rest of my career. *Calendar Girl* did not perform, and I had no idea that in "the industry" it had been my one big chance. In the eyes of the major Hollywood studios, this was my chance to show whether or not I had what it took to be a movie star, and I had failed the test. Utterly.

I was still in my early twenties, starring in one of the most popular shows on TV. I would not have believed that my one and only shot at movie stardom had come and gone. It was probably a good thing for my morale that it took years to realize that such a major career crossroads had come and gone in the blink of an eye without my having even realized it.

To this day, I think I made the right choice as, fortunately, the other two scripts I turned down were never made. It's not like I turned down the lead in *A River Runs Through It* for *Calendar Girl*. As disappointed as everyone associated with the film was by the box office performance of *Calendar Girl*, it does seem, many years later, that it struck a chord with at least a couple of filmgoers. I know this because I still have people tweeting me about that movie, and quoting lines from it, so I know somebody saw it! "I just want to lay on top of you and see where it goes from there," anyone?

Piccadilly Circus
London
W1J 7BX

Fans develop a very intimate relationship with the characters in their favorite TV shows. Perhaps it is because the time spent together occurs in your home, with our images beamed directly into your room. Whatever the reason, *90210* fans across the world felt they had a real relationship with me . . . or nice guy Brandon Walsh, anyway. That's the only way I can account for the insane level of fame I achieved playing Brandon. My sister, Justine, was living in London as the show really heated up, and Eddie Michaels and I were planning a trip to the United Kingdom to do press. *90210* was wildly popular there, as it had been pretty much from the start.

My sister was worried. "It's going to be nuts here for you, JP. The British fans are psychotic. I'm seriously concerned for your safety." We went back and forth a bit, and then she had an idea. "You've got to do something. Just give Ayrton twenty pounds a day to act as security," she advised. Ayrton was my sister's Brazilian boyfriend. He was a big, ripped guy—perfect for the job.

All was well during our visit—Ayrton stuck close, and there were no incidents. Until one afternoon the four of us were wandering through Piccadilly Circus and ran smack into a girls' soccer team. They appeared to be fourteen or so, a very dangerous age. I cringed as they spotted me and began squealing. I knew an attack was imminent. They pointed at me and started running as a pack directly toward us. There were probably twenty-five of them, all wearing matching uniforms. In their blue zip-up jackets, they looked like an army of Smurfs coming at us.

Panicked, I looked over at Ayrton, who was watching the girls approach with wide eyes. He looked back at me and said, "I'd run if I was you, dude." Some security. So that's exactly what we did. We took off and the pack of soccer girls chased us all the way through Piccadilly Circus, screeching the whole way. A couple of quick rights and lefts and into an alleyway, and we lost them. It's not that I was in mortal danger—nothing of the kind—but for some reason, since watching *A Hard Day's Night* when I was a kid, I just always thought it wise that when screaming teenage girls are chasing you, you run.

Magic Mountain
Valencia
91355

Since the first episode of the show I had been bugging Aaron to give me a shot to direct. It was something I was very interested in exploring, and I knew that this show might be my best chance. I also understood that learning television, and the television business from Aaron Spelling, was an opportunity that I needed to maximize.

So much of the entertainment business is having the ability to recognize opportunities and capitalize on them. You have to be able to keep building on your successes. And I have found, you have to do these things for yourself, regardless of how many people you employ to help you. You always have to stay on top of your career, your finances, everything. Always keep your eye on the prize. Every time in my life that I let my focus waver, it has led to disaster.

Toward the end of the third season of the show, Aaron gave me my shot at directing. When I think back on it, I have to wonder exactly what Aaron was thinking, handing the reins of his hit show, his baby, to a twenty-four-year-old punkass actor kid. It happened to be a very complicated episode titled "She Came in Through the Bathroom Window." We shot on location at Magic Mountain. I had hundreds of extras, cameras mounted on roller coasters, and car chases . . . plus, I had *Burt Reynolds* in my episode. It was awesome!

Burt was the man. At the time he was starring in *Evening Shade* and had been a big star forever. When he strolled up to me in his cowboy boots and leather-sleeved jacket to say hello, I was thrilled!

"Mr. Reynolds. This is the very first television episode I'm directing and I can't tell you what an honor it is to have you here. Thank you so much. It's so great to have you."

"Yeah . . . I've done some directing here and there myself," he drawled. "Let me give you some advice."

I was all ears. "What's that?"

"You do a first take, right? And it looks okay?"

"Right," I said, not sure where this was going.

"Wanna do another take? Just tighten up a little bit. That way, you'll have something to play with in the editing room."

"All right, Burt. Thanks!" What Burt was telling me was how he would like to be shot. And that is exactly how I shot him. But in a way, he was absolutely right, and it's a piece of advice I carry with me to this day. The more pieces of coverage you have in the editing room, the better. Burt was a smart guy, a real professional. Later on, his good buddy Dom DeLuise would show up on *90210* as well.

Seven shooting days later, my first episode was complete. I've got to hand it to the crew and rest of the cast . . . every one of them was totally supportive, professional. Ultimately, they wanted me to succeed and for my episode to do well, so they helped me out, and it all came together very well.

Aaron liked it, too. The next season he gave me two episodes to direct, and three in season five. Then I directed five episodes in seasons six and seven. By the time it was all said and done, only one other director had directed more episodes of *Beverly Hills 90210* than I had. I also produced the show in seasons six and seven and executive produced the show in seasons eight and nine. Once again, I was looking to maximize my opportunity with Aaron and learn as much as I could from him.

AFTER MUCH DELIBERATION, it was decided that the cast would all graduate at the end of the third season. Of course, that meant a two-hour "Graduation" episode and the infamous "Donna Martin Graduates" episode, which, to this day, is a huge fan favorite. In the show, Brandon leads a triumphant march across the football field. We were all supposed to be chanting, "Donna Martin graduates." Of course, it took less than thirty seconds for me to change it to "Donna Martin masturbates." Everyone else immediately picked up on it, and suddenly everyone was chanting along with me . . . "Donna Martin masturbates . . . Donna Martin masturbates. . . ." There were several other iterations as well, but I'll leave those up to your imagination. I knew they were going to go back and reloop this dialogue anyway, so it was pretty irresistible. I mean, the writers had to know that would happen, right? It was one of the funniest moments we all ever shared, and I led the charge . . . Donna Martin masturbates! Pure comedy!

Naturally, for high school graduation, we shot on location at Torrance High School. This particular show was a big deal, in part because we had to use hundreds of extras. The day before, production had brought in bleachers to use in the shoot. Our security team arrived early on the day of filming and swept the area. They found two homemade bombs hidden where we would all soon be sitting. That caused an uproar, and the team took them off and detonated them somewhere safe. The incident held up production for a few hours while authorities were notified and everyone ran around double- and triple-checking everything. Finally, they declared the area safe.

Apparently, *90210* had worn out its welcome at Torrance High.

Tucson
85757

Appearing in the movie *Tombstone* on my hiatus was a fantastic opportunity. I loved the script as soon as I read it, and I couldn't resist doing a western costume drama, which was so different from what I was doing at my day job on *90210*. The cast was all-star: everyone from Kurt Russell as Wyatt Earp to Val Kilmer in an unforgettable portrayal of Doc Holliday, to the veteran of a hundred westerns, Sam Elliott himself.

I played the supporting role of Billy Breckinridge, a sweet and naive young man hopelessly out of place, tagging along with a gang of vicious bad guys known as the Cowboys, identifiable by their blood-red sashes. The movie shot on location around Tucson with a huge cast. Along with all the movie stars and "film" actors in the cast, there were a couple of other faces that were recognizable from television. Thomas Haden Church, playing his first role as a mechanic on *Wings* at the time, was there playing a Cowboy, as was John Corbett from *Northern Exposure*, almost unrecognizable behind his beard. The three of us were immediately tagged the "TV guys" and became fast friends.

On Friday, after only one week of shooting, the film's director, Kevin Jarre, was replaced. All the actors were informed that a new director, George Cosmatos, would be coming in on Monday. That weekend, the entire cast and crew speculated endlessly about this bombshell. What's going to become of this film? What about my role? What's going to happen to *me*? The first instinct of many of the actors was to quit, as they felt the film had been Kevin's baby. His brilliant script and the opportunity to work with him were the main reasons we were all there. There was such a hubbub over his firing that Sam Elliott called a meeting in his room for the actors to air their grievances.

Michael Biehn, who played the gunslinger Johnny Ringo, was particularly upset by the change; he was a close friend of Kevin's. During the meeting in Sam's room we were all drinking whiskey. After a few shots, Michael really let loose. "I'm not doing this fucking movie with anybody but Kevin," he said, and "This is bullshit," and on and on.

"Michael," I said. "You don't know George. Why don't you wait and see what he's like on Monday? It might all work out."

Michael stood up and walked across the room toward me. "What did you say . . . kid?"

Emotions were running high, and all his frustration and anger was suddenly redirected at me. The menace in the air was unmistakable, and the hair on the back of my neck literally stood up. I rose as he drew near, bracing for a fight.

"Whoa, whoa, hold on there, boys," Sam Elliott jumped in. "There'll be no fighting in my room." He soon got everyone sorted out and reseated. Thank God, because I didn't like where that confrontation was headed.

George Cosmatos, director of *Rambo* and *Cobra,* arrived and took the helm. All of the actors ultimately stayed on board. Production on what was destined to become a classic film moved ahead, and I had the time of my life. Tommy, Johnny, and I headed out on the weekends and just tore up the greater Tucson area. Maybe because we appeared in people's living rooms every week, the three of us were always the first to be recognized when a bunch of the cast was out together. Kurt Russell, a major star for most of his life, told me that growing his big mustache was the best disguise ever . . . he could

walk around anywhere and no one paid him any attention. He was
having a great time.

As for the TV guys, bad behavior abounded all around. We used
to come staggering home in the early morning and grab a few hours
of sleep, then drag ourselves out to the pool with a cooler full of beer
on weekend mornings. The cast and crew hotel, where we all stayed,
was an older three-story building, built around a central courtyard.
The door to every room faced the courtyard, with the pool in the
center. As the morning wore on, the three of us would observe numerous women doing the walk of shame out of various cast and crew
members' rooms. We would wildly applaud them as they passed us,
hungover and wearing last night's dress, on the way to their cars. The
ladies did not appreciate it.

In terms of work, I had several big scenes. One of them in particular was extremely dramatic. On my big day, as we were preparing to
shoot, most everyone was just standing there, waiting for "Action!" to
be called. I was laughing and horsing around with some of the crew,
bullshitting about what we'd all done in town the previous weekend,
waiting for my name to be called. Sam Elliott came striding over,
grabbed my arm, and pulled me aside.

"What do you think you're doing?" he growled.

"Me? What do you mean, Sam?"

"You're fucking around. You are in a big scene! Prepare!" Sam was
a very intense guy. A real perfectionist. He was appearing in the scene
with me, and he expected me to give my best. What he saw was a
young actor fooling around, and he gave me one hell of a talking-to.
One I haven't forgotten to this day.

I have always enjoyed friendly relationships with everyone on film
and TV sets. I really enjoy people on the crew, who tend to be an
adventurous bunch, and I like hanging out with them. But this re-
minded me that I was on set to do a job, an important one, and this
was my day to shine.

In this pivotal scene, my character was supposed to be absolutely bereft. Beyond brokenhearted. As Billy, I said something like, "You killed my friends, and if I was something, I'd kill you myself," knowing there was nothing I could do. I needed to be at the top of my game, not just jumping in and out of the scene. Prepared—all there—mentally, emotionally, physically.

I must thank a true professional for calling me on my bullshit. The scene worked, and I have Sam to thank for it.

On the Set
Van Nuys
91406

Oh, man, to this day I remember that red dress. Every year, at the beginning of the season, we would do what was called a gallery shoot for *90210*. This would give the PR team enough shots of everyone to distribute throughout the year. It was basically a very long photo shoot that every main cast member was required to attend. We usually used a warehouse in an industrial park across the street from our studio. In many of these warehouses they shot "adult films." (As I previously mentioned, we were in the heart of Van Nuys, porn capital of the world.)

As the years rolled on, Shannen, Jennie, and Tori became ever more competitive. They formed an eternal triangle where someone was always on the outs, and that "someone" changed all the time. Jennie and Shannen were both very strong personalities, while Tori would careen back and forth between them, freezing the other one out.

It was a dynamic that plays itself out every day in every sorority house and cheerleading squad in the country . . . this one just happened to be on the TV set of a hit show, and therefore of great interest to the general public. It was silly little stuff, not huge feuds, as reported in the tabloids. We all loved the show, and we all loved the work we were doing. And any backstage squabbles were never brought into the work itself.

Then, of course, there was the drama with their boyfriends. Us guys were the spectators who had been watching it for years. Nick Savalas, actor Telly's son, was trouble. Nobody liked the fact that he was dating Tori. Unfortunately, he was around for a long time. It was obvious he was mistreating her. We definitely saw some telltale signs. One night Luke jumped right into Nick's face about it. Tori and Nick made all sorts of headlines for a New Year's Eve brawl. He was not a popular guy when he showed up on set. We knew she deserved much better.

Shannen, meanwhile, moved on for a time to Dean Factor, a cosmetics heir to the Max Factor fortune. At one point Dean gave her several no-limit credit cards and she moved into the Four Seasons Hotel. On her hiatus, Shannen shot a movie called *Blindfold* and had a fling with actor Judd Nelson, one of the original "Brat Pack." She was using Dean's credit cards to take Judd out to clubs . . . it wasn't going to end well. And it didn't.

Jennie had a serious musician boyfriend, Dan, and they were briefly married for a couple of years. Meanwhile, there were still plenty of little petty dramas.

On season four, we gathered for the annual gallery shoot, and it got completely derailed in the wardrobe department. There was one really stunning bright red dress on the rack, and all three girls insisted on wearing it because it would stand out the most in a photograph. Each of the three girls was determined to wear that dress, and no one was backing down.

Naturally, this meant that the guys had to sit around for hours, waiting for the girls to settle on who got to wear the red dress. A wonderful producer named Betty Reardon and our executive producer, Paul Wagner, were brought in to settle the situation. Betty was the best; she could magically smooth over matters like this between the girls—something she was called upon to do on a frequent basis. It was agreed at the end of the day that none of the girls would wear that particular dress, and other suitable outfits were found for all three of them. And I do mean the end of the day, since these negotiations took hours and hours.

Nothing new here. By this time, I knew quite well how these things tended to go. I always showed up to events like this with a bottle of scotch. I knew there was going to be plenty of sitting around, so why not take advantage of it? Luke, Brian, Ian, and I would pull up some chairs, pour ourselves a drink, and shoot the shit. There was no sense fighting it or trying to talk sense into the girls. We stayed the hell out of it and took the opportunity, with all four of us in one spot, for a leisurely talk.

I HAD SEEN plenty of Shannen's boyfriends come and go. Even so, I was shocked when she showed up for work one morning and said, "Oh my God, so I got married over the weekend." Very casual, in the same tone she might use to mention she'd gone out and gotten drunk at the Cabo Cantina on Friday night. *90210*'s resident bad girl marrying Ashley Hamilton after only a few weeks of dating was big Hollywood news; all the shows and gossip magazines went nuts. The new couple appeared on *Saturday Night Live* together at the height of their notoriety.

Back at her regular day job, however, things were starting to crack. Her sudden marriage was a very Shannen thing to do. That girl lived minute by minute, doing exactly as she pleased, never worrying about consequences or crying about the past. Of course, it was also not a surprise that the marriage was quite stormy and ended in a matter of months. The crew had a pool going for how long the marriage would last . . . the over/under was ten weeks.

It was around this time that Shannen started showing up late to work. Not every day, but pretty consistently. And not fifteen minutes late—in L.A., that's considered on time. I'm talking at least an hour. However, there was never a day she didn't turn in a good solid performance . . . once she got to the set. Shannen by this time was quite a notorious tabloid fixture for her late-night partying and fights in clubs. In my opinion, none of that media storm bothered Aaron. He was a firm believer in the adage that there's no such thing as bad press. He had Hollywood's resident bad girl starring on his hit show, and he didn't mind what she did outside of work. He did mind when her antics began holding up production.

All issues aside, Shannen could deliver, and I always believed much of her success could be credited to her innate ability to live in the moment. Although this trait got her into trouble in real life, it served her well as an actress. However, it did not serve the needs of the show and FOX; and at the end of the day we were not just "hot young stars." We were employees, just like everybody else.

On the Set
Van Nuys
91406

In my travels, I have learned that a surprising number of people have a wildly inaccurate idea of what it's like to star in a television show. They believe that in Hollywood, you roll into work at noon, have lunch delivered from a fancy restaurant, shoot until four or five, then cocktail hour begins. Then it's time for your massage, and the cocaine dealer and hookers arrive . . . or so the fantasy goes, anyway.

The reality of working on a show in Hollywood is waking at 5:30 in the morning to drive to work and arrive by 6:30. You're at the studio until seven or eight at night, and then you drive home—and do homework for the next day's work before bed. Sure there's some downtime during the day, but you usually spend it going over lines, talking to the writers about something, having a fitting . . . there's always something that needs doing. This is what you do every day as the star of a one-hour weekly show. Certainly that was the experience for me. Shooting 22, 26, 28, and eventually 32 episodes per season is a long grind, a real marathon, and it takes stamina and professionalism to get through it.

So we all knew going in that we were going to be there at least twelve hours every day. That was fine, part of our job, and we all liked our jobs. That meant all of us, crew included. However, when one person on the team is disrupting everything by showing up two, three, four, and even five hours late every day, it quickly throws the whole balance off, resulting in major problems for the other hundred employees affected by those actions. When you work on a television show, you're all in it together, meaning the cast and crew and everyone who contributes in any way. Everyone needs to be prepared to show up and create scripted television shows that people want to watch. Bottom line. It takes time and effort to do that correctly.

I was on set all day, every day for nine to ten months out of the year. Many of the other characters parachuted in and out—Luke might work a couple of days, Jennie would show up four days that week, Ian had three days on set this week . . . meanwhile I was there seven out of seven days. Week in, week out.

As the fourth season wore on, Shannen was talked to on numerous occasions. I am sure Aaron himself no doubt had a word with her somewhere along the line. At some point, though, I imagine she thought the producers were just crying wolf, because they gave her *numerous* chances. Eventually, the pressure started to build. The phone calls started pouring in to Aaron from everybody. There was an overriding feeling on the set that we needed to get back to work. Frankly, Shannen and her habitual tardiness could no longer hold an entire show hostage. The show was a big hit, but its success could easily be derailed at any time, most certainly by bad behavior. None of us wanted that to happen.

To his credit, Aaron knew when to pull the plug. He gave her many chances over a long period of time, but once the decision was made, it was a swift and tough call. Her firing had absolutely nothing to do with any of her supposed "bad behavior" outside the show . . . drinking, fighting in clubs—all that stuff didn't matter. It was that she was holding up a very important production and affecting the lives and livelihoods of many people. Aaron called Shannen's agents and told them that she was being written off the show. She stayed for another couple of episodes so they could write her character off—Brenda left for London to study at the Royal Academy of Dramatic Art. Off she went, supposedly for a year, and though she would be referred to often in the future, she never returned to the show.

And just like that, the actress with whom I had worked so closely and shared so much for four years was suddenly gone. Our show would have to be a different show moving forward. Life in the zip code was about to change.

West Los Angeles
90024

The first time I read the script, the film was called *Sang Froid*—French for "cold blood." It was a dark comedy to be produced by Michael J. Fox's company. My role would be that of Cosmo, a bookie who reluctantly becomes a hit man.

The film was shot on my hiatus after the fourth season. The rest of the cast was stellar: Peter Riegert, Robert Loggia, and my love interest, Kimberly Williams, from the *Father of the Bride* blockbusters. Janeane Garofalo had a small part, as did Josh Charles, who now, years later, has a huge hit on the TV show *The Good Wife*. The writer/director, Wallace Wolodarsky, went on to do groundbreaking, amazing work on *The Simpsons;* even Michael J. Fox made a cameo appearance.

The experience was fantastic. It was one of those sets where everything is fun; we all got along so well and had such high hopes for this project. During filming, OJ Simpson drove right by our set in the infamous slow-speed Bronco chase, and we had to halt shooting because of the sound of the helicopters overhead. Of course we all gathered around the TV for the rest of the day to watch history in the making.

Sadly, *Coldblooded* was a great movie that nobody saw. When it debuted, it was very well received by audiences on the festival circuit and was a big hit at Sundance. It was an independent film that got bought by Polygram but, because they were having financial problems at the time, the movie quickly disappeared. It went straight from festival hit to home video.

It was just another swing and miss for me in the movies, but that's show business. Fortunately, I still had my day job.

Chicago
60601

I stayed in touch with only one person from my real high school class, a guy named Drew Strazman who worked as a stockbroker in Chicago. One night I found myself in Chicago and stopped by to see him. He was playing some music I really liked.

"What's that you're listening to?" I asked.

He handed me the CD of a band called Barenaked Ladies. "These guys are huge back home in Canada," he said. I took the CD home and was immediately hooked; they had a unique sound. When I saw that the band was playing House of Blues in L.A., I made it a point to go, and made my way backstage when it was over. Ed Robertson and Steven Page had been friends since their Toronto high school days; they were now a band of five. "I'm having you guys over!" I said on the spur of the moment. "When can you come to my house . . . now?"

Sure enough, late that night their tour bus wound its way through the hills to our house, and Christine and I had a late meal with the band. "You guys are great," I said. "Why don't more people know about you in America? You need to shoot a music video and get some exposure here." This was the mid-1990s, and MTV was still breaking out hits through music videos.

They told me that they had shot a few but didn't like the results. They had spent a lot of money on what they felt was a substandard product, and they couldn't get on MTV or VH1. Now, I'd had a few drinks. "I'll shoot your next video, and you'll love it," I boasted. "And I'll walk it into MTV myself!" They had nothing to lose; they took me up on my impromptu offer.

So on my way to Nova Scotia to shoot *Love and Death on Long Island*, I stopped in Toronto and in four or five days I prepped, shot, and edited *The Old Apartment* video for Barenaked Ladies. We had a minuscule budget, about $35,000. Still, it turned out very well. When I had finished acting in my own film, I stopped in New York for one night on my way back home to L.A.

I went into the Viacom offices and showed the video to the creative team at VH1. "This is the music video I directed for my friends, Barenaked Ladies. They're huge in Canada. I hope you'll want to put it on your channel."

"This video is great," they agreed. "We'd love to." Simple as that! The very first Barenaked Ladies video appeared on TV in America. The video was instrumental in the band breaking through; they finally got some airplay on American radio, and even made an appearance at the Peach Pit After Dark. As for me, I was nominated for a MuchMusic Video Award later that year. The MMVAs are a big deal, Canada's annual video awards show that attracts musicians from all over. All kinds of American music acts attend and perform there each year. My youthful hubris paid off, and I had some new friends in the music biz.

Beverly Hilton Hotel
Beverly Hills
90212

It was that time of year again—the annual fancy rubber chicken dinner event. The Golden Globes were much more fun when I was a nominee! This was actually my second nod for Best Performance by an Actor in a TV Series (Drama)—the first had come in 1993. In 1995, my girlfriend, Christine, and I walked the red carpet and headed into the huge ballroom. We found our seats at the big round table and sat down. Christine, who was currently playing med student Harper Tracy on *ER,* immediately fell into conversation with Heather Locklear, who was making a big comeback as Amanda on *Melrose Place.* The room was starting to fill up. I glanced over to my right and there were my old buddies, Brad Pitt and Johnny Depp, standing there chatting. They'd met back in the day on *21 Jump Street*—because *every actor* our age had been on *21 Jump Street*. Forget six degrees of Kevin Bacon! Trust me, every actor in Hollywood around my age passed through *21 Jump Street* at some point . . . or *90210*.

I stood up and walked over. "Guys! What's up!" I was delighted to see them both, as I hadn't talked to either of them for a while. Brad was nominated for his performance in *Legends of the Fall;* Johnny had been nominated for Best Performance by an Actor in the comedy/musical category, for the quirky *Ed Wood*.

"Let's go to the bar and have a drink!" I said, and of course they didn't need much arm-twisting. It was just like old times. We all went outside to have "a drink" and wound up standing together, laughing, chatting, telling jokes, and knocking back quite a few cocktails for the next hour or so. We had a great time laughing about the old days. Who would have thought back at the beginning that all three of us would be at the Golden Globes, much less nominated in the same year?

None of us won our category. Dennis Franz of *NYPD Blue* beat me out that time around. Still, it had been a fantastic evening. The best thing about the Golden Globes is that it's pretty much the one place everyone in the industry shows up, giving actors a chance to catch up with old friends, because there's no Celebrity Café in Hollywood where all the famous people go. A successful actor is all over the world at any given time working on various projects, which makes staying in close touch difficult, particularly back then, before we all started carrying computers in our hands.

Montecito
93150

My buddy KC and I had been racing cars for Toyota for three years during every moment of spare time I could muster. We were doing quite well when Ford contacted me to see if I wanted to start racing Mustangs for them in IMSA (International Motor Sports Association)—an association that is no longer in business. (Now it's called Grand Am.) During my first year I was given a Mustang Cobra R to drive, which the Ford Company had just released. We were one of the fortunate few teams that got the new model right off the line. It was fantastic to be part of a factory effort like that. I loved the excitement and fun. I started running the Grand Sports Division, and it was great.

KC raced with me for the first half of that year with Ford. This was a whole different kind of racing—endurance racing. I had my eye on racing in such premier events as the twenty-four hours of LeMans, and starting to race in the Grand Sports Division was the first step toward those big goals. The races were three hours long. One driver goes for an hour and a half and then the other driver runs for an hour and a half, with one pit stop in the middle of the race to change drivers, change tires, fuel the car, and so on. Unfortunately, we weren't doing well. I got called into a meeting with the executives at Ford one day. "Jason, we want to partner you with a stronger driver because we need you to be running up front." It was up to me to let my partner go.

This was a terrible moment for me. KC was—and is to this day—a dear friend. We had started this journey together and had had so many good times the past four years. Not to mention that he was a very good driver. However, Ford was paying the bills, so I had no choice. Needless to say, the breakup of our partnership put a strain on our friendship, a relationship I valued a great deal. It took some of the shine off my excitement. This part wasn't fun—at all. Much to his credit, our relationship survived and he is now godfather to both my kids.

My new partner was a guy named Andy Pilgrim, an absolutely phenomenal driver, one of the best in North America. Andy and I hit it off immediately and were quickly successful. Andy was an incredibly fast driver, but, more important, he was a great teacher. He was smart and a good communicator and knew everything there was to know about cars. He taught me so much about how to become a better driver and how to race faster. He and I remained a solid team over the next three years.

Being constantly under the glare of the spotlight was no longer fun. Every cast member of the show needed a place to go and hide, and racing was my hideaway. Well, one of mine. Driving around one weekend, I found a very cheap house in Montecito that was a foreclosure. I snapped it up dirt cheap from a bank in Texas. Those kinds of deals just don't happen now, but it was possible back in the mid-1990s.

I paid next to nothing for that house, for good reason. It was a wreck. I convinced the brother of a friend of mine, a very talented guy named Tom Lawler, to come out from Boston and live in the house as he redid it, room by room. He was a master tile- and woodworker and whenever I wasn't racing or working, I would drive up on weekends to help him out.

Together we gutted that house. I hired a separate company to redo the kitchen, but Tom and I did everything else ourselves. I have always loved manual labor, even as a housepainter back in Vancouver. For me to go work on my own house was very cool, a real labor of love. I seemed to wind up with all the demo work, while Tom was an artist.

We also installed gorgeous redwood wainscoting, and when the renovation was over, I had created a beautiful, peaceful weekend retreat, which was just what I needed. Christine and I spent as much time as we could there, given my insane schedule. I was racing whenever I could, so when I was in town, it was the perfect escape for me to just drive up to Montecito.

I was at work all the time, like a hamster on a wheel. When I wasn't on set, I scouted acting and directing projects to do during hiatus. I made all kinds of PR appearances and commitments for the show. On the weekends, I either jumped on a plane and headed to the racetrack or drove down to the new house for the weekend.

By this time Christine and I had five dogs! I'm sure it was illegal in Los Angeles County, but we did it anyway. The dogs loved the house in Montecito, which was set on a full acre. In addition to Swifty, who was very happy in this pack, we had a wolf hybrid, a little red pit bull named Friday, a pug named Dempsey, and a Boston terrier named Bobby Orr. Guess who named him?

By this time, it was impossible for me to be anonymous in public. The possibility of becoming so famous had truly never entered my mind. The fame I achieved was a strange by-product of the work I enjoyed. There had simply been no way to prepare for the constant public attention. The kind of attention we were all receiving would drive anybody crazy.

Racing and fixing up my house: these two respites kept me sane. Driving required intense focus. Manual labor allowed my mind to wander and daydream a bit. The mental states were polar opposites, but they both gave my mind a much-needed break from work and from my increasing fame.

Detroit
48226

Nearly every time one of the cast members appears on a talk show, and they show photos of us from the early days, everyone pokes fun at the high-waisted "mom" jeans, the popular style we all wore back then. That look certainly didn't age well!

Pepe Jeans London approached my agent, Nick, with an offer for me to represent Pepe Jeans. The company was founded by a young designer who originally customized jeans out of his stall in London's famous Portobello Road market. He and his brothers soon expanded into several stores, and then a warehouse, eventually becoming London's most popular designer denim brand. In the '90s, the company made a big international push to conquer America and the world.

It seemed like a regular straightforward business deal—an ad campaign for jeans—but once Bruce Weber came on board, it became a very artistic project. The week that I shot with Bruce in New York was an unforgettable experience. Bruce was a master, an incredible artist This was far more than a photo shoot—we spent an entire day in a Tribeca loft, another day in a Brooklyn park, yet another in a downtown neighborhood taking photographs and filming for a commercial.

I'd taken part in many photo shoots by this point in my career, but this man worked on an entirely new creative level. To be his subject was a privilege, and the results, mostly due to his artistry, were amazing. Images of me were on billboards all over the world. The commercials, containing snippets of such people as Allen Ginsberg, reading his own poetry, were incredibly high end and artistic for a denim campaign. I felt lucky to be a part of it.

As part of my deal, I made a number of appearances around the world, promoting Pepe Jeans. There were screaming girls at malls around the country when I showed up at department stores, but these appearances were very well managed and controlled, and I enjoyed them.

It was now full-on *90210* hysteria. Jennie and I made a brief appearance at the Detroit Auto Show, where we stood onstage at the Joe Lewis Arena to present a check from Chrysler Motor Corporation to a charity. All we did was carry one of those oversized checks out and hand it over to an official; we didn't even speak. Fifteen thousand people in the arena went completely nuts. The screams and applause were deafening. Every kid there went wild at the sight of us! Jennie and I were stunned by the huge wall of sound coming toward us.

That kind of cacophonous roar was electric. It was almost a physical force hitting us; I had never felt anything like it in my life. At that moment I understood what it must be like to be a rock star. I also understood why so many rock stars become addicted to drugs—they want to re-create the high of that feeling *all the time,* because it was amazing. It was the coolest. There were several events like this in my life during that period and, in hindsight, I wish I had enjoyed them more.

Unfortunately for me, I was cursed with the awareness that often the candle that burns the brightest only burns half as long. I never wanted to be someone who burned so hot that I would quickly flame out and turn to ash. I didn't want to be superfamous and all over the place for five years, and then disappear. I was in this job for the long haul. I wanted to lay the groundwork for a successful career as a working actor for decades to come. This kind of heat and intensity could only burn out, and all I could do was hope and pray that I would still be there, intact, when it did.

Beverly Hills
90210

The fifth season of the show marked the arrival of Tiffani Amber Thiessen. Tiffani brought a breath of fresh air to *90210*. She played Valerie Malone, a childhood friend of the Walsh twins, who was forced by family troubles to move into their home. Valerie was a great character: troubled, duplicitous, in and out of fights with the girls and romances with the guys. We hit it off right away and became great friends from the start. The chaos, drama, and negativity that had taken over the set magically vanished. Tiffani brought an entirely new attitude to work, one we hadn't witnessed for a while. Tiffani wanted to be there. She was helpful and professional and came up with creative solutions to any issues that arose. She was friendly with everyone. I could not have been happier with the positive energy she brought to the show, and I hoped she would stay for a long, long time.

The fifth season was chugging along without incident. Shannen's departure didn't hurt our ratings one bit. In fact, they kept getting stronger. We were all in a good place with the show, and the days, weeks, and months seemed to just disappear. But we were all coming to the end of our original contracts, and talk of renegotiations was on the horizon. Was everyone staying? What kind of raises could we ask for? There were a lot of questions, and a lot of uncertainty. Then two things happened that changed the course of the show completely.

Chuck Rosin, our show runner, had a heart attack. He would be okay and, with help, be able to finish the season, but he would not continue after the fifth season.

And Luke Perry was leaving the show.

Luke left the show ten episodes into the sixth season. When he told me he wasn't going to sign again, I was disappointed on both personal and professional levels. He was a very good friend, and we had experienced a lot together. I hated to see him go, though I could certainly understand that he was creatively frustrated and didn't want to become typecast. I directed Luke's final episode, a very dramatic show where Rebecca Gayheart's character was mistakenly killed by her father's hit men. I was going to really miss my friend.

Beverly Hills 90210

Playing the moral compass of the show, I was never going to get the big dramatic scenes. Brandon would never have the big crazy story arcs or drunken or drugging scenes (except for the U4EA episode, when Emily puts a hallucinogen in Brandon's drink, with disastrous results).

Every show like *90210* needs a moral anchor, and that was my character. Of course there were disagreements and creative conflict with the actors and the writers, but a certain amount of creative discord is healthy. We had just enough to keep everything interesting and everyone on their toes.

Aaron knew I was becoming restless with my role and looking to do something different. He told me, "You can be as involved as you want to be with this show." He had previously been gracious enough to provide me with directing opportunities, but I had my chance to understand the full picture when I became a producer of the show on seasons six and seven. The cast were still in their college years, so we were able to continue many of the through lines that were still happening.

"Great," I told him. "I'm going to be completely involved." And I jumped in with both feet. I was going to learn from the master. How many people are given the opportunity to attend the Aaron Spelling School of Production? Once again, I tried to maximize every opportunity. Not to discount the old man, Aaron was very canny; he knew it would keep me around for another year or so. He was well aware that I was champing at the bit to do more.

And that's just what I did; I would produce the show in seasons six and seven and direct five episodes in each of those seasons as well. Those were busy seasons. I would lighten the load in season eight, only executive producing the show alongside Aaron.

Van Nuys
91411

While I was acting as producer, one of my duties involved sitting in on casting meetings for the extensive list of guest stars who came through the show. Years before, I'd been the one to campaign for Stephanie Beacham to play Dylan's mother. Now I brought in my old buddy, Paul Johansson, to play John Sears, the head of a fraternity that Ian's character, Steve, was trying to join. He was perfect for this role: a big jock, just like he was in real life. Pauly Shore stopped by for a flash, playing an unruly bar patron—just like when we were kids on *21 Jump Street*. Was this typecasting?

One day we sat in a long casting session for the part of Carly Reynolds, a single mother of a young son to play Ian's love interest. A young woman named Hilary Swank was by far the best actress in the room; she was head and shoulders above everybody else we saw that day. I knew she would be the right fit, so it was surprising to me that I had to fight to have her brought back for a callback. Nobody else seemed to have seen what I saw. I forced the issue, and she came back to read for us again.

After her callback, the other producers still weren't convinced. We had seen every young actress in town, and, as far as I was concerned, it had been a waste of time. We had the perfect person ready and waiting. Finally, I convinced everybody—including Aaron. Besides being a very sweet girl, Hilary was extremely committed to her craft. Right from the start, her character was written for a one-season arc, so she left us after sixteen or so episodes. As devastating to her at the time as leaving the show might have been, it was obviously no reflection on her talent. She went right from us to the independent film *Boys Don't Cry,* and we all know what happened next.

Now that I was a producer on the show, I also wasn't afraid to take more chances as a director as well. Aaron had very specific tastes and liked things a certain way. But I was a young director, and I was trying to find my way and play with all the toys that were at my disposal. So I would imagine scenes and allow myself total creative freedom, and that would lead me to requesting all kinds of crazy equipment from our production manager, JP. Techno cranes, hot heads, huge packages of prime lenses, Cartoni heads—I would ask for them all.

"Whoa, whoa, slow down there. What do you think this is?" I was definitely *that guy* on the show. JP would call me into his office and say, very confidentially, "Jason, the Cartoni head? Aaron doesn't like that. He hates Dutch angles—so don't do it."

"Trust me. I got this, I got this." I wasn't worried; I had my vision. I did a few Dutch angles—turning the camera to a 30- or 45-degree angle—only when I felt they were really needed for very specific shots. I loved them; they were popular back in the film noir days of the '30s and '40s. The first time I ever put a Dutch angle in, Aaron and I were sitting in his office together, side by side as usual, screening my episode. He did a double take when he saw that shot, then cocked his head and gave me a look.

"Hey, Jason . . . something's wrong with the TV!"

"Ahh, come on, Aaron. That worked!"

He shook his head, but he trusted me. He must have, because at the end of season seven, I directed probably the most famous episode in the history of *90210,* when Donna Martin finally lost her virginity.

Awkward! I just looked at Aaron when he gave me the news. "Really, Aaron? Really? You're giving me this episode to direct?"

"Who else? Who else am I going to give it to?"

Oh, man. Kid gloves dealing with that situation! I was hyperconscious that this was Aaron's daughter, Aaron was my boss, and I must handle the situation respectfully. I did my best, even as I did such tasks as choosing Tori's costume, which was a bustier with garter belts . . . she put on quite a show for her "first time"!

Donna losing her virginity was a national obsession; the story line had taken on a life of its own. To be in charge of this particular episode was more ironic than anything else, as I had never figured out the huge fuss that Americans made about anything and everything to do with sex. Canada, along with the entire rest of the world, was far more open and liberal in this regard than the puritanical States. I could not relate at all to the big deal young people here made of losing their virginity. My bigger challenge was to figure out a way to make the encounter as erotic as possible without really showing anything. *90210* was seen by millions of young people and aired at 8:00 P.M., so its content had to be G-rated. Sexual activity could only be implied.

As was our tradition, I took my director's cut over to Aaron's office to discuss it. I sat next to him and tried not to squirm as we watched an episode featuring his only daughter losing her virginity on-screen. I was beyond nervous. Aaron chewed on his pipe the whole time but said nothing. Finally, we came to the end—Donna and David are really going to do it! I cut to candles burning and the screen goes black for a moment before the titles started rolling. I waited with bated breath for Aaron to speak.

"Very tasteful, Jason, very tasteful," Aaron finally pronounced. And that was that. He signed off on it. I was very glad that particular directing gig was over.

Aaron was a great showman. He taught me so many things, and one was the value of keeping it simple. That's where some of his greatest successes lay. He told simple stories, with pretty people in beautiful

clothing, in aspirational locations . . . he had a regular formula he followed, and it worked for him. He lived by his rules producing television, and there was no arguing with his success.

Aaron had come back big. He was well into his sixties and already
insanely rich when *90210* began, a time when I think a lot of industry
people expected him to just hang up his hat. He had made one hell of
a comeback, and I was honored to be a small part of it.

Sunset Strip
West Hollywood
90069

Christine and I had been fortunate for nearly five years to actually live a pretty normal life in our house in the hills. Everyone at the local grocery store knew me; same with the local deli and wine store. All the stores plus a dry cleaner were in one convenient location. It was a great little neighborhood, and when I stuck close to home I was in my own space, where no one cared who I was or what I did. There didn't tend to be packs of paparazzi chasing people around and camping outside their homes in those days, at least not outside our home. They would be at the clubs and restaurants, but they didn't stake people out the way photographers and TMZ do now.

The seventh season was ending—along with what had been a happy and rewarding relationship between Christine and me. Things had been unraveling for a while. It was clear we were drifting in opposite directions. Ultimately, Christine and I just wanted different things out of life. She was perfectly content with our arrangement—and don't get me wrong, we had a great life. Still, I knew that someday I wanted to have kids, and that was something she was not interested in. I knew I had to make some changes to my life in order to eventually have a family life, and while I was nowhere near ready for kids, I was ready to at least start considering the possibility.

A conversation I'd recently had with my friend Michael Budman was on my mind. Michael is one of the owners of the Canadian clothing company Roots and a brilliant businessman. He, like many of my friends, was considerably older than I; he told me one day that the best move he'd ever made was to wait until he was forty to have kids. "Your twenties are for fucking around; your thirties are for making money; your forties are for raising a family and devoting your life to your children," he told me. Wow, write that one down and remember it. A road map to life right there . . . if you don't get derailed somewhere having too much fun.

The actual split with Christine happened just as summer hiatus began on *90210,* and it was extremely unsettling for me. She remained in our house for a few months until she could find something new, so I moved out and rented Peter Weller's place on the Sunset Strip while he was in Italy making a movie. I was living in this rented bachelor pad alone and starring on a hit TV show. This was really the first time I took advantage of that situation vis-à-vis dating, because up to that point I usually had a steady girlfriend. I didn't do a film on hiatus that summer. Instead, I found quite a few short-term girlfriends at the SkyBar in the Mondrian Hotel, which was very handily within walking distance.

My life on the eighth season of *90210* was quite active, to say the least, and for a while I was out every night. I can't lie—it was fun as hell, at least until the novelty wore off. But underneath all the fun and nights out and beautiful faces, I felt adrift. At sea. No bearings in this rented house and no one to come home to. I was searching for something new that year, and it was more than a bit unnerving. I had no compass. Eventually, Swifty and I returned to our house in the hills, but it wasn't the same. We were leading the bachelor life, but the reality wasn't as enjoyable as the idea of it.

At one point I flew to Las Vegas to see the guys from Barenaked Ladies play at the Hard Rock Hotel. After their performance, I jumped on the bus with them and rode with the band to San Francisco, where they had another gig. I slept in one of the coffins on the bus and had a great time catching up with everybody.

When we arrived in San Francisco, we pulled up in front of the Phoenix, a very rock-and-roll '50s-style hotel located in the heart of the Tenderloin District. I got off the bus and stood in front of the building with the driver, waiting for the rest of the guys. Ed, the lead singer, got off the bus and nodded approvingly. "Cool! The Phoenix! I fuckin' love this place!" he said, and hurried around the corner and into the lobby to register. Then Steven, the other lead singer, came off the bus. He took one look around the funky neighborhood and the old hotel and said, "The Phoenix. The charms of this place are lost on me." He shuffled dispiritedly around the corner and out of sight.

There's a movie, right there! is what I thought. I wished I had a camera. These two guys, who have known each other since high school, had been on the road together for fifteen years, and they could not be more diametrically opposed in everything . . . except for their music.

The seed of an idea was planted. Over the months it would change, grow, and expand and become close to an obsession.

Spelling Manor
Holmby Hills
90024

Actors," Aaron Spelling used to lament. "I put shoes on their feet and they walk away from me." Aaron was very much a father figure. He had nurtured me and supported me and been my champion from day one; I knew I owed him a lot. We had been working together for years, extremely closely for the last three while I attended his impromptu "production school." I was well aware of his feelings about the actors he had cast over the years, often in star-making roles, who left his shows to pursue other projects.

Still, it now felt inevitable that I, too, would leave *Beverly Hills 90210*. I loved and respected Aaron with all my heart, but I had to go. I'd gotten my first television series, *Sister Kate,* when I was nineteen years old, a time when most kids are fooling around in college. The kind of sudden and unexpected fame I achieved just a few years later on *90210* was a trauma. The potential was there to really harm me later in life, because fame can stop cold much of a person's development.

My experience on *90210* is why I think I got along so well with race car drivers and other professional athletes. We were all approaching thirty years old, but acted and felt as if we were eighteen. Professional athletes tend to be very young in many ways, and I'm not just talking about their chronological age. They've been big stars since their teens, and that's just about where much of their growth and education stopped. It's the same thing with many musicians and actors. I fit in great with my actor friends and athlete friends, but as far as being a real live regular human being—no. I had a lot of catching up and growing up to do.

Whether you're a five-year-old kid, a teen actor, or a middle-aged guy on the set, if it's a big successful show, people do things for you. There's always somebody there to feed you, to fetch your car, to find your clothes, to throw out your garbage. You simply don't have to take care of yourself. All the mundane daily stuff is done for you. That isn't real life, and I was savvy enough to realize that. I knew I needed to break out of what was, in many ways, a gilded cage.

I had been working on the show for so long and hard that most of day-to-day life had passed me by. I had no idea what was going on in the greater culture. Work was how I clocked everything . . . in terms of what episode I was on, which show I was directing, what film set I was on. I had worked close to twenty hours a day for years.

Those years went by in a blur. We were shooting what we called "double-ups." Three times a year, we brought in an entire second crew to shoot two episodes simultaneously. The actors bounced back and forth between the two sets. This resulted in our whopping thirty-two shows per season, an unheard-of amount of material. This was why the cast and crew affectionately referred to the show as the Sausage Factory. We churned out tons of sausage, efficiently and fast.

Plus, I was racing—I was still under contract to Ford and MCI. I was very seriously burning the candle at both ends. *90210* and racing and red-eyes and travel and promotion and casual dates. There was a swirl of activity around me all the time. Still, I knew there was another world out there. Some of my friends had regular, nonindustry jobs and were climbing the corporate ladder. They had all read books I hadn't read and argued passionately about politics I didn't understand. I wanted to rejoin the rest of the human race. I was a part of everyone else's pop culture, but I had no idea what was going on. Staring thirty in the face, I knew it was time to make a change.

On a purely practical day-to-day level, I also didn't like what the show had become. The plots had become quite nonsensical. I had

begged Aaron to stop the show. It was way past time to marry everyone off and pull the plug, but he wouldn't hear of it. I made up my
mind. The show could go on forever, but I was leaving. By that time I
was on a one-year contract, and when my contract expired at the end
of the eighth year, this time I was going to go. I set up a feature film
to direct about Barenaked Ladies that would occupy the entire next
year of my life. When he got the news, Peter Roth, who was the head
of FOX at the time, tried hard to get me to stick around for the ninth
season. I resisted, which wasn't hard. It was much tougher when I had
to talk to Aaron face-to-face.

Aaron summoned me over to the Manor on a weekend to discuss
my decision. He had just undergone double hernia surgery, so he was
in bed, and I actually had to sit at his bedside for this very difficult
conversation. I had a sinking feeling in my stomach the entire time, as
it was a painful discussion for me to have with a man who had treated
me so well. I felt so guilty that I wound up making quite a few conces-
sions. He talked me into staying for the first four episodes of the ninth
season. But that was as far as I was willing to go.

With *90210,* Aaron and I had created something great together.
Now here I was, telling him I didn't want to do it anymore. That I,
too, was walking away. It breaks my heart, looking back, that I was so
insensitive. It's hard for me to have to face the fact that I hurt someone
who was so good to me. I can't even try to fix it, as he's no longer here.
I wish I could talk to Aaron one more time, and tell him how sorry I
am that I left, but, more important, that I'm sorry I let him down personally and hurt his feelings.

Aaron had been through this scene many times before; he took my
leaving well and didn't reproach me. He stayed my friend, of course,
and we continued to see each other quite a bit. But our relationship
was never the same. It couldn't be. That was my fault. At that time
and that age, I was just too focused on my own wants and needs. It is
only now, as an older man looking back, that I can understand how
much my defection must have hurt him. To have caused that man one
minute of pain is one of the biggest regrets of my life.

Beverly Hills 90210UT

In retrospect, I should have stayed on that show until they dragged me off in a body bag. Until Brandon died in the Beverly Hills Nursing Home of old age. I was a complete dumbass not to stay until the bitter end. Whatever damage was done to my acting career in terms of typecasting was irrevocable. A year or two more of playing Brandon would not have mattered in the least. I should have socked away as much money as I could before transitioning into the next phase of my career. By the way, that's what I would tell any actor, ever, period. No discussion: if you're lucky enough to be on a hit TV show, don't leave until they kill you off. You never know when, or if, the next one's coming.

I also wish I had stayed because I believe the show should have ended differently. I think we owed the fans the ending many wanted and seemed to think was coming. There had been a classic episode where faced with a choice between Dylan and Brandon, Kelly said, "I choose me!"—which led to endless hours of comedy between Jennie, Luke, and me afterward. However, in the intervening years, particularly after Dylan left the show, the story arc made it pretty clear that Brandon and Kelly were written in the stars. Meant to be. Now, of course, given the benefit of hindsight, I should absolutely have stayed on the show and had Brandon and Kelly live together happily ever after. That's the way it *should* have ended.

Aaron was a good guy and he stayed on good terms with most of the actors who left the show, myself included. My leaving was a big blow; having Luke return a few months later for the last two seasons gave the show a much-needed boost after eight years. Our great friend Paul Wagner had been diagnosed with esophageal cancer and Luke was particularly close to him; I believe that the chance to spend time working closely with him was a large factor in Luke's decision to return. Paul was a great man whom we sadly lost a few years later.

My last day of work was oddly anticlimactic. No one gave me a cake or going-away party on my last day of *Beverly Hills 90210*. On the fourth episode of season nine, I shot my last scene with Daniel Cosgrove, a new addition to the show playing the role of Matt Durning—my replacement, basically. We were the first scene up in the morning, so I was in and out. I said my good-byes right then and there, then everybody else moved along to the next scene. For them it was just another day at work.

I walked to my dressing room for the last time, grabbed a box of stuff, went out to my car, and drove off the lot. I was a bit sad to be leaving this group of people with whom I'd spent the last nine years of my life. But it was time for other adventures. I was going on the road with my racing buddies, and then on tour with a rock band!

Vancouver
V6A 4H6

By this time, I had closed the doors of my race team, Triple Caution Racing. Andy Pilgrim went to drive for GM, and I was fortunate to get picked up by a team out of Toronto called Multimatic Motorsports. I drove for the next two years with a partner named Scott Maxwell, another very talented driver, one of the best in North America. He taught me a lot. We raced not only Mustangs but did a lot of damper development work for other teams. We were also running a GTS1 Mustang program. That was a tube-frame 780-horsepower race car. We got a third-place finish at Laguna Seca in the 1997 season in that car against all the big European GTS1 teams. The two of us did very well together.

I'd met a guy named Greg Moore at a charity softball tournament in Indianapolis a couple of years before. He was a very young driver, barely out of his teens, from my hometown of Vancouver. After meeting in the dugout, we were fast, forever friends. He loved *90210* and every now and again I'd thrown in a word, or gesture, directed specifically at him, which absolutely delighted him. Freed from my day job, Greg and I, along with some other guys on the Indy car circuit, did some traveling, saw the world, and had some unforgettable times. Racing was my world, I couldn't ask for better friends than these guys, and I loved every minute of it.

When summer rolled around in 1998, I went on tour with the Barenaked Ladies for a couple of months. My original impulse was to shoot a documentary about this incredibly popular band from Canada, the hottest thing ever up north, but coming to the States and playing to six or seven people in a bar someplace. The dichotomy interested me, as did the whole idea of breaking through in America. I wanted to juxtapose them playing in front of huge stadium crowds in Toronto, then five people in a bar in Phoenix. That, I thought, would make for a funny movie.

Things did not turn out as planned, however; by the time I was out on the road with the band they were extremely popular; they had the number one song in America! It was quite an adventure and I wound up with more footage than I knew what to do with. I parked myself in an editing suite in Vancouver and started cutting.

Franklin
37064

An offer came along for the role of a very bad guy in a movie called *Eye of the Beholder*. It was director Stephan Elliott's follow-up to *Priscilla: Queen of the Desert*, though this was a much darker project. The film starred Ewan McGregor and Ashley Judd. It only required a quick one-week shoot on my part, and the movie was filming in Montreal, a place I love. Stef was a crazy Australian genius and I was anxious to work with him.

Working with Stef and Ashley (whom I was very quickly calling by her last name only, Judd) was a pleasure. In the film I played an evil guy who came in, beat up Judd, shot her up with heroin, and pretty much messed everybody up. This was a role as polar opposite from Brandon as I could find, and I relished playing a villain.

Ashley and I were passing the time one day on the set, idly talking about her love life. She was single at the time and bemoaning it. She knew I raced cars and mentioned a driver she'd seen in an interview on TV. She thought he was really cute, a Scottish guy named Dario Franchitti. I said, "I know Dario!"

"No way!"

Of course I knew him, through Greg and everybody else. "You'll see, Judd," I promised her. "I know him."

A few months later I had business in Los Angeles and while I was there threw a party at a restaurant on the West Side called the Buffalo Club. I happened to know that both Greg and Dario were in town and invited them . . . along with Judd. She met Dario at the party and that was it. They were a wonderful match, both supersweet people. Both excelled in extremely high-profile professions but were very private people at heart. Dario spent much of his off time in his native Scotland; Ashley didn't live in L.A., preferring her homes in Kentucky and Tennessee. Growing up in a famous family as she had, she felt so much of her life was already out there for the world to see. She guarded her personal life carefully. I was happy to see two friends so happy together.

Sometime later I found myself in Nashville on Indy Racing League business. I was very taken with this southern city, and the surrounding green countryside was absolutely gorgeous. I gave Judd a call to see if she wanted to meet for dinner, and she insisted that I come stay at her house instead of a hotel. It was at her beautiful home that I was introduced to one of the great pleasures of the South. Judd had a well on her country property that produced the purest, most delicious water. The bar in her living room had a water line that drew directly from the well straight to a jet in her wet bar.

"Try this," she said, and mixed me a drink of bourbon and water.

Now, I'd done my share of drinking—vodka, scotch, rye—but I wasn't familiar with really good bourbon. To me, Maker's Mark was as fancy as it got! I had never known anything like this magic elixir. Blanton's is a small batch, single-barrel bourbon. Phenomenal! Ashley had her own supply, straight from the maker, with her own personalized label. That was quite impressive.

I may have changed Judd's life by introducing her to Dario, but she absolutely returned the favor by introducing me to Blanton's.

The filming of *Tombstone* was one of the best movie-making experiences I've ever had.

My personal trainer Eddie gave me a convincing boxer's body.

When I moved from Toyota to Ford my first assignment was to go race in the Australian round of the World Rally Championship for them. We started 38th and ran as high as 16th before crashing out on day two of the three-day event.

I introduced three-time Indy 500 champion Dario Franchitti and Ashley Judd at a party I threw in Los Angeles. They got married the next year. Here they are at that party with Greg Moore and his girlfriend.

The 98 car, the "Flexi Flyer." It was fast but never handled right.

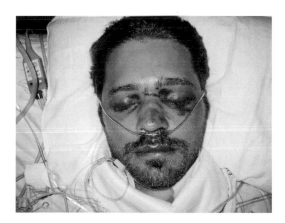

My near-fatal crash changed not only my face, but also my life.

There was no room to think about acting when I was in a race—and I loved it.

Our spectacular wedding was a one-and-only experience—
for everyone.

Sharing a laugh with
Bradley Cooper.

Our wedding invitation.

After the children came along I was never the same again.

Ava, my cover girl.

Dashiell, my little cowhand.

This is me and my sister, Justine, on the beach in Vancouver circa 1975. You can see why people thought I was a girl. . . .

The kids loved Deckard as much as I did.

Naomi and me with Swifty. We made quite a team.

Toronto
M9C 5K5

In November of 1998, a producer friend named Peter Simpson called me to talk about a movie he was putting together called *The Highwayman*. I told him I couldn't even consider it; I was right in the middle of cutting my film. "Ah, you need a break. It'll be good for you to get away for a month. Come to Toronto, shoot this movie for me. At least take a look at the script."

The project was a crime drama about a bank robber named Breakfast and his partner, Panda. Panda was a wild, crazy sociopathic criminal. As I read, I thought to myself: Coulson! What a brilliant idea! I called Peter and said, "We should bring Bernie Coulson in to play this guy! I've known him my whole life, it'll be perfect! We'll have a blast!"

Peter didn't exactly jump on this suggestion; in fact, he sounded strangely reluctant. Looking back, I think it's because, living in Toronto, he knew more about Bernie's situation than I did. We had all been young and wild in the '80s and early '90s. L.A. life was full of temptations. Plenty of people I knew skated right on the edge in terms of partying. Drugs were all around, all the time. Some people did too much, some didn't. Some people could turn the party off, some couldn't. It was dangerous, all of it, though it hadn't seemed so at the time. We were cool, it was fine, everything was under control, of course.

I hadn't personally seen Bernie for quite some time. The last I'd heard, his agent and a couple of friends had pretty much grabbed him, forced him onto a plane to Vancouver, and called his mother, saying, "We're sending this guy home to you for a break. We can't deal with him anymore." But that was years ago; I was sure he had pulled it together by now.

Peter tracked Bernie down, made a deal, and soon enough we were reunited on set. I was so happy to see him again. As filming wore on, we had a great time, just like old times. Of course, we were still young guys and we liked to have fun and party after work, but nothing that got too out of control.

While I was shooting *The Highwayman* with Bernie, I got a phone call notifying me that my uncle, my mother's younger brother, had suddenly died. David was only ten years older than me. He'd had a massive heart attack and was dead before he hit the floor. Because we were so close in age, we were unusually close for an uncle and nephew while I was growing up. In fact, just before *The Highwayman,* he'd spent a week with me in Los Angeles just hanging out.

He was a very fit guy, an avid runner, and only forty years old. This was a horrible shock. Fortunately, being in Canada, I was able to attend his funeral. Back on the set, I was not quite in the same partying mood. But work was going fine, and I certainly didn't see anything in Bernie's behavior to alarm me at all until one morning when I got a call from our driver.

The usual routine was that the driver picked Bernie up at his hotel, then came to pick me up, then dropped both of us off at the set. One day, in the middle of the week, I was sitting in the kitchen, drinking coffee at six A.M., waiting for the driver. He didn't show up. The phone eventually rang, and it was Pete. "I'm at the hotel and Bernie's not here. What do you want me to do?"

"What do you mean, he's not there?"

"I've been looking everywhere. I finally had someone from housekeeping check his room. He is not on the premises."

"All right," I said. "Come and get me, then we'll go find him together."

The weather was bitterly cold, and the winds were brutal that winter. There was no reason to be outside unless you had to be. Still, we figured we might find Bernie on Lower Yonge Street, the drug-buying area of town. Sure enough, we drove around for just a few minutes and then saw him, buying crack from a dealer on the sidewalk, standing there in plain sight, not hiding.

Pete pulled up next to the two guys. I jumped out of the car and grabbed my friend. I snatched the bag out of his hand and threw it to the ground and then shoved Bernie into the backseat. It was like a kidnapping.

"What the hell are you doing?" Bernie said in an injured tone as we drove away.

"Bernie, what are *you* doing? It's six thirty in the morning, man, and we are supposed to be at work right now! What. The. Hell?"

I was not pleased, but I was mainly more surprised than anything else. We'd been having such a great time. There was no one like Bernie when it came to having fun. By the time we got to the set that morning he had me laughing about the whole thing. I was convinced it was just one more crazy, over-the-top Bernie escapade. This guy and I had been through so much together. "Blood Brothers," right?

But then it happened a couple more times during the six-week shoot. This was where Bernie was in his life. He apparently could not even get through a month or so drug-free. My feelings changed from surprise to annoyance to real anger as the problems on the film mounted. Finally, I just wanted the shoot to end. Bernie did finish the job, barely, and then returned to his regular life in Vancouver.

A few weeks later my phone rang. Bernie was at a Western Union office in the seediest part of downtown Vancouver. He needed cash, or some guys were going to break his legs because he owed them some money. Or something like that; I barely listened. I broke into his story.

"How much money, Bernie?"

"Five hundred dollars. I have to have it today, Jason, right away!"

"Here's the deal, Bernie. I'm going to wire you five hundred dollars right now. And in return I want you to lose my phone number."

As promised, I sent the money, and Bernie lost my number. That was fifteen years ago, and I haven't spoken to him since.

Ucluelet
VOR 3A0

Imet a businessman through some Canadian friends who was developing a piece of property on the west coast of Vancouver Island. I headed out there one day with a bunch of other people to check out what he was building. He was constructing ten cabins right on the waterfront in a tiny fishing village called Ucluelet, just south of Long Beach, a popular tourist destination. The location was amazing, offering access to a private beach. My old friend Terry David Mulligan and I bought one of the cabins on the spot. We owned our cabin, but when we weren't using it, the cabin went back into the rental pool in a standard kind of operation.

The plans were for a resort, with ten cabins and twenty other lofts overlooking a boardwalk next to the water. Each cabin was completely self-contained with several bedrooms and bathrooms on two levels, full kitchens, washers, dryers, and so on, where families could come stay for a week or two in the summer. It was a charming, quaint little development. When I was a kid, my parents used to take us to vacation on the west coast of the island, back when you could camp out on Long Beach. It was much more remote then; there are rules and regulations prohibiting camping there now, but I'd always loved that area and remembered those days. This group of guys appeared to be a solid group to do business with. All the cabins got snapped up, as did the lofts.

There was a man in charge of the entire development. He was also in charge of the finances, making sure all investors got their money at the end of each month, that the taxes were paid, and so on. All the details of running the resort fell to him. A year into our project, it became painfully clear that he was not operating the resort the way it should have been. Too many customers were leaving, not having had a good experience, and certainly were not coming back. There were numerous complaints. The group of homeowners, myself included, had to remove him from the operation. We brought in another man to hopefully turn things around.

However, many of the original investors had gotten cold feet. They just wanted to walk away from a bad investment and move on. They simply stopped paying for their cabins and let the bank foreclose on their mortgages. I saw a good opportunity here. I approached my father and told him that I had a chance to pick up a bunch of the cabins at a greatly reduced rate and eventually start operating the place myself. By myself, I really meant my father, as I couldn't possibly manage this project remotely. Fortunately, he agreed, and as more and more properties at the development came up for sale through foreclosure and tax liens, we snapped them up. Eventually, I owned twenty units.

Things looked very grim our first couple of years, and I couldn't blame most of the original investors for cutting and running. But today, fifteen years later, Terrace Beach Resort is a thriving business. We've had families come to vacation there year after year after year. It's been an excellent education in the hotel business, but it's also been a great opportunity to work closely with my father. He oversees everything there, and, trust me, with the weather on the west coast of Vancouver Island, there's plenty of upkeep to keep him busy.

Santa Monica 91411

While I was still in Vancouver, I had been contacted by Marcy Poole, who ran the Movie of the Week department over at FOX, about directing the first in what they hoped would be a series of movies for them. They wanted to take old film noir titles from the 20th Century FOX archives, update the stories, and remake them as Movies of the Week.

This was the perfect job for me. I was a huge fan of film noir and to have an opportunity like this just handed to me was such a gift.

Kiss Tomorrow Goodbye was a remake of the classic 1942 film *Moontide*, starring Jean Gabin, Ida Lupino, and Claude Rains. Nick Lea, from FOX's hit show *The X Files*, starred as the main protagonist. FOX was looking to promote him at the time. He played the main character of Dustin, a Hollywood producer who wakes up on the beach one morning, near the body of a dead girl, but remembers nothing and is soon being blackmailed. I was able to cast my good friend Holt McCallany as Minnow, the antagonist. I took a small role as his best friend.

Directing that movie was a challenge but it was also a lot of fun. I had twenty-four days to shoot this Movie of the Week, and a real budget—something like four and half million dollars. Those days with plenty of time and money are gone. The locations were gorgeous, including the Sunset Strip and posh beach houses, and the sound track was amazing. The film itself turned out very well, and then, just like that, FOX decided to get out of the Movie of the Week business. There was never another in the series, or another Movie of the Week. It was the end of an era.

Via Marghera
Rome
00185

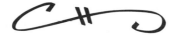

I finally finished editing *Barenaked in America* and returned to L.A., but I felt restless and antsy and uncomfortable there. I wasn't sure what I wanted next, but somehow I no longer loved L.A. as I had from the day I arrived as a teenager. Something was off. Looking back, I see it was me. I hadn't been quite myself for a while. I was especially restless now that I had finished my huge labor of love—the documentary. I dyed my hair a bright chicken-fat yellow. Not for a role, just for a change. Not my best look.

When May rolled around, it was time for the American Music Awards again. I was asked to present an award and headed out to Monaco with my racing buddy Scott Maxwell. Pamela Anderson hosted the show that year, and after it ended, it was time for the official postshow banquet, which was hosted every year for the participants by Prince Albert.

Then Scott and I moved on to the main reason for our trip. We headed to London for the inaugural Gumball 3000, a three-thousand-mile illegal road race crisscrossing Europe, founded by a filthy rich British entrepreneur/race car driver, Maximillion Cooper. There were about fifty of us drivers participating. I was in a (borrowed) Lotus Esprit V8. Billy Zane, with whom I'd shared a memorable scene in *Tombstone,* drove an Aston Martin. We took off from London and drove to Dover to get ourselves and our cars on the ferry to Calais. We rode across the English Channel, then got in our cars and raced to Le Mans. We swung through Paris and stayed in castles at every stop, having an absolute blast.

It was then on to Monaco, then Rimini, Italy. In Rimini, the Gumball 3000 crowd took over an entire hotel. Imagine fifty guys and gals, rowdy as hell, having been racing nonstop for days and days, arriving at the lobby of the most beautiful and ornate hotel in the country. A bunch of us grabbed the scooters we all carried with us for pit stops and drove them into the lobby. Then we started racing up and down the Grand Staircase, drinking heavily of course. It was extremely bad behavior and we were politely asked to stop a few times, but no one paid any attention, until the security guy pulled a gun on us and started screaming in Italian that it was time to go to bed. The party stopped abruptly.

The accidents on that trip were epic. Scott and I were professional drivers, adept at driving 150-plus miles an hour. But these other guys? They were just a bunch of millionaires driving $300,000 Ferraris and wadding them up right and left. They simply had no business driving 180 mph and it was fortunate that no one got badly hurt. The participants in this particular race didn't care if they wrecked—they could just buy another car. It was a very memorable event . . . Scott and I drove the wheels right off that car to the end. As the years passed, the annual race became more and more elaborate, the celebrating more and more out of control. I'm just glad I survived.

Toronto
M9C 5K5

During production on *Kiss Tomorrow Goodbye,* I got the news that *Barenaked in America* had been accepted into the prestigious Toronto International Film Festival. We would be in the Reel to Reel section and have our world premiere at the famous Winter Garden Theatre. This was a huge honor (or should I say *honour*) for a first-time documentary filmmaker. I was quite humbled. But there was also much to do and much to prepare for. So it was easy for me to keep on working and ignoring the things in my life that I knew needed to be dealt with at some point. Work and racing were the ultimate distractions. I could feel the pressure really starting to build, which made it even easier to keep losing myself in my work and professional commitments.

Being back in Toronto with Barenaked Ladies was, as always, a fantastic time. The boys were in rare form as we introduced our film to a packed house at the Winter Garden Theatre. The Ladies were riding a huge wave of success and it was an exciting time.

We sold the film to the Shooting Gallery and got a theatrical release, an amazing feat for a small documentary. It was extremely successful for a documentary at that time and place, and it did very well for me, the band, and for all parties concerned.

New York
10012

After the film festival, I headed to L.A. for a few weeks, and later to New York for a directing job. I was directing an episode of Tom Fontana's new drama *The Beat,* about NYPD cops. I'd always felt happy and at ease in big cities. Of course I enjoyed L.A., which had been my home since 1987, but I had always loved New York City. Ever since my first visit when I went there as an eighteen-year-old visiting to screen test for the feature film *Heartbreak Hotel,* there was just something about that place that got under my skin. The noise . . . the energy . . . I've always felt at home in New York.

Days on *The Beat* set were long and all-consuming. There's a lot of pressure directing in Manhattan. On Halloween Sunday I was relaxing, sitting in the corporate apartment the show had put me up in, settling in to watch the Marlboro 500 being run at the Fontana Speedway back in California. In a horrible irony, I watched on TV as my friend Greg Moore's Indy car flipped and slammed upside down onto a wall at 200-plus mph and he was instantly killed. All the hours he'd spent watching me act on TV . . . and now I'd watched him die on TV, for real. I was in shock.

I couldn't make sense of it. I sat in stunned silence. Just three days before the race, Greg and I had talked on the phone for thirty minutes while he was driving up to Cultus Lake to go fishing. He'd ended the phone call by saying, "Talk to you Sunday, after the race."

Even though I had known him only four years, we had been very close. We had spent days and hours and weeks in each other's company and traveled the world together. You name it—we'd been there and done that—together. Racing cars, having fun. I had watched him grow from a twenty-year-old boy to the outstanding twenty-four-year-old man he was when he passed. The very next morning I had to be back on the floor, calling "Action" and "Cut." Adding insult to grievous injury, I couldn't attend Greg's funeral. The service was held on Thursday, and I was in the middle of directing a TV show. I had known since I was five years old that no matter what, the show went on. Greg would have understood—he loved hearing about my "other" jobs acting and directing. It was heartbreaking for me to miss gathering with his many other friends and colleagues and mourning together. But there was no way around it.

Greg's death affected me deeply. And it forced me to come to the realization that I was wasting my life. Life is short. Oftentimes, too short. I needed to make some changes in my life that I had been putting off and now was the time to do it.

Los Feliz
90068

I returned from directing *The Beat* a rather beaten man. I had just lost one of my best friends and I was coming home to deal with many of things in my life that I had been running away from. These were dark days.

Regardless, none of this excuses me from what happened the night my buddy Chad Cook and I went to the Wiltern Theater to see Chris Cornell. After the show, we went backstage, had a couple of beers, and then headed home. It was a very mellow evening. I was just nearing Chad's house when I wrecked. As was my habit in those days, I was driving too fast and carelessly on winding canyon roads. *Boom!* My Porsche crashed into a telephone pole. The second the spinning stopped, I looked over at my friend.

"Chad. Are you okay?"

"No, no, my arm's busted." He was grimacing in pain.

I pulled out my cell phone and dialed 911 to get an ambulance there as fast as I could for him. I could not have felt worse. The ambulance arrived to take him off to the hospital while I, of course, had a little discussion with the police. I wasn't even worried about a DUI; I wasn't drunk. Then I failed my roadside sobriety test, and they took me to Rampart Division for a blood test. Result: .10, two-tenths over the limit. Not exactly hammered, but legally drunk. And not only would I be charged with a DUI, but given Chad's injury, it would be a felony

DUI. I would eventually get transferred to the Hollywood sheriff's station where I had to stay for a few hours. My friend Cheryl came to bail me out. There was a lone reporter outside the jail as we exited in the very early hours of the morning. The reporter worked for one of those daily evening shows that report on happenings in entertainment, like *Access Hollywood* or *ET.* I stopped and made a brief comment, which was a mistake. I should have learned that it's best to remain silent in a situation like that. There was really nothing I could say anyway; it's not like I was trying to justify anything. I knew quite well it was a stupid mistake and the ending of a very, very bad year. There were quite a lot of legal issues to contend with here. I had to face up to a number of facts, and none of the realizations was easy or fun. My actions were hurting not only myself, but others as well. I lost my license for a year, and at some point, I was going to have to do some sort of jail time, but what worried me the most was my green card status. I wasn't a U.S. citizen, and this very foolish episode could jeopardize my entire future. I had come back here to L.A. to get it together and very foolishly just created an even bigger mess for myself.

And magically, out of nowhere, there came a project that would take me far, far away . . .

New York
10112

Side Man had just won the Tony Award as Best New Play and was heading for the West End in London. They were looking for someone to take over the role of Clifford that had been vacated by Andrew McCarthy. The offer came to me, just after my DUI, with the added bonus of costars Edie Falco, Frank Wood, Angelica Torn, Kevin Geer, and Michael Mastro (the original Broadway cast). I would spend the first three weeks of the year rehearsing in New York before heading to London for a twelve-week run. What a fantastic opportunity to run away from my problems! Giddyup!

Needless to say, I jumped at the chance to flee L.A. and say good-bye to the past millennium.

I arrived in New York just after New Year's and began rehearsals on Side Man. I was working with director Michael Mayer and the stage manager every day in a rehearsal hall just off of Times Square. I was staying in midtown, on 56th Street, and would walk to and from rehearsal every morning and night. The more time I spent in the city, the more I wanted to stay. I told you I was getting really good at running away from my problems. And the DUI was a big one. I had lawyers that were handling all the legal aspects of it—it was the practical side of it that I found daunting. Having lost my license for a year made getting around L.A. very difficult.

So in my time off from rehearsals, I started to look around for a place to live. And lo and behold, I found one. I bought a huge loft in Tribeca in a very cool building, where every loft took up an entire floor. Each floor in the elevator was keyed, meaning the elevator opened into individual apartments. Imagine the best New York apartment you can: this place was it. I decided I was going to make the move to New York City. Once again, not a well thought-out decision. But my mind was made up. I was staying and that was that. I called my business manager and told him to sell my house in L.A., my house in Montecito, everything. I was done with L.A.

You know that old saying, "If I only knew then what I know now"?

6-8 Wellington Quay
Dublin
Dublin 2

I arrived in London at the beginning of February, met the rest of my cast mates, and began rehearsals in earnest.

Immediately after I arrived, John Hurt and his girlfriend, Sarah Owens, invited me to Dublin to attend the Irish Fashion Awards, which I had never heard of. They were taking place on a random Sunday night and I thought, *Why not?* What really tipped the balance was the chance to see Andrea Corr again, from the Corrs. Not only had the Corrs performed at the Peach Pit After Dark, but we'd had a very friendly encounter the previous year at the World Music Awards and I knew she'd be at these awards. I wanted to see her again, so I grabbed an overnight bag and flew to Dublin, checked into U2's hotel, the Clarence, and headed to the awards ceremony. The place was simply raging.

Everybody was there. It was nuts. Everywhere I turned there were more famous faces than you'd ever see at the biggest event in the States. All the guys from U2 were there. Mick Jagger was there. Naomi Campbell was there. Every single hot model in the world, apparently, was there. Then the whole British contingent was there: Jonathan Rhys Meyers and every other hot young English and Irish actor. The turnout was absolutely amazing. These were fashion awards, so all kinds of designers were winning various honors that night. I hadn't realized fashion was quite so big there . . . maybe everyone just wanted to go to Dublin for a party!

During the awards intermission, most of the audience left their seats and milled around in the lobby. I spotted Andrea standing at the bar and made a beeline for her, saying, "Hey, how are you?" She looked me up and down and then said in a chilly tone, "I didn't know you were going to be here," and then looked back down into her drink. I was taken aback. "Hmm . . . well . . . okay then. See you later." Suffice it to say, she wasn't thrilled to see me in the least. Wonder what I did to illicit that kind of response? Oh well . . .

When the awards were over, everybody headed back to the Clarence. Sarah, who was Irish, apparently knew every single person from her home country and introduced me to the guys from U2 . . . our hosts, as it were, as we were all staying in their hotel. They were very low-key, cool guys. We were all drinking in somebody's room when Sarah grabbed my arm and we raced to the elevator, headed upstairs to a very high floor, and followed some people into a huge suite. And there, right in front of me, were Mick Jagger and Jerry Hall lounging on a bed, passing a joint back and forth. Mick's jewelry designer daughter, Jade, was wandering in and out along with a couple of other creative/design-type people. Sarah flopped into a chair in their bedroom and said, "Hey, Mick, pass it around."

"So sorry, luv," he said. Then he got up and handed the joint to me; I took a drag and passed it back to Mick . . . And there I was, smoking up with Mick and Jerry. I certainly wasn't in Lynn Valley anymore.

It was a fun weekend in Ireland, but I had an opening night to prepare for.

Covent Garden
London
WC2H 9HB

Side Man covers thirty years in the life of a New York jazz musician as seen through the eyes of his son. It's a beautiful, haunting piece written by Warren Light. We moved into the Apollo Theater at the end of February and started technical rehearsals. Theater could not be a more different sort of undertaking than working on a television show. They're night and day—hard to even compare. There's no second take on stage, which forces an actor to be absolutely present, in the moment and engaged with the other actors during every show. There is nothing more gratifying than to live those moments for an audience every night. Theater is the purest form of what actors do. I was excited to get back to the stage, something I hadn't done in a decade.

The show opened and the reviews came in and were better than we expected. The British critics can be a tough crowd, and for the most part they liked *Side Man*. Our houses were good and we, as a company, were all working well together and I was becoming friends with my fellow cast members.

Outside the theater was another matter. I had now run 5,400 miles away from my troubles in Los Angeles and yet they were still troubling me. I was wound way too tightly and was acting erratic.

The Apollo Theater is in a part of the West End that is surrounded by pubs, and our play would finish around 10:40. Meaning I would be outside the stage door signing autographs around 11:00. Just when all the pubs in the area kicked out all their patrons. And said patrons, feeling no pain, have fun hurling insults at the actors signing autographs outside the theaters. Especially one from television. Especially one from *Beverly Hills 90210.*

Now, a normal thirty-year-old wouldn't let things like this bother him. Nor should he. But all of a sudden I found myself excusing myself from my fans to chase after drunken hooligans looking to get into fights. Something was very wrong with me. I needed to start taking responsibility for my actions, clean up the messes I'd made, and start growing up.

Covent Garden
London
WC2H 9HB

After the show ended one night, I exited the theater with the rest of the cast onto Shaftesbury Avenue. We were headed to Joe Allen's in the heart of the West End for a drink and dinner, which was a tradition in the London theater world. At just after eleven P.M., all the pubs were closing, and the streets were crowded with people streaming out. Two exceptionally pretty girls, both wearing pin-striped blue business suits, crossed directly in front of me; they were obviously a bit tipsy. I caught a whiff of perfume as they walked past. I smiled; I loved British girls!

We continued on our way to the restaurant, and a few blocks up the avenue I suddenly saw the two girls again, standing across the street. The beautiful blonde was holding her head in her hands, clearly a bit worse for the wear, as her friend looked on. "I'll see you there!" I told my friends and darted across the street. I walked over to the girl and asked, "Are you feeling all right?"

"Do you know if there's a toilet round here?" she wanted to know.

"I'm sorry, no, I'm from out of town." We talked for a bit and I learned that her name was Naomi Lowde. She had recently graduated from university and shared a flat with a friend in London. She'd been out with her friend from work all evening, and they were returning to their office to pick up a computer that night. As for me, I told her my name was Jason and that I was a housepainter. After a few minutes, I said, "I need to catch up with my friends for dinner . . ."

"Okay," the girl said, "see ya later." I hesitated for a moment—Naomi was one of the most stunning girls I had ever seen—then said good-bye. I walked around the corner and proceeded up the street. A minute later I heard, "Wait, wait!," and there was Naomi's friend running up behind me. I waited till she caught up with me. "Naomi wants you to have her phone number," she said, out of breath, as she thrust a scrap of paper with a London number into my hand. I was charmed; it was all very playful and high schoolish.

"Great, fine, I'll give her a call," I said. Then, Mr. Cool Guy that I was, I turned another corner or two and realized I was suddenly, hopelessly lost. I had no idea where Joe Allen's was located or where my fellow cast members might be. This was strange, especially since I have always had an excellent sense of direction in any city I found myself in. I wandered around in confusion for a while, made a few false turns, and then headed toward the biggest major intersection I could see, hoping it was Covent Garden. If I could get to Covent Garden, I could find the restaurant.

I turned another corner onto a random London street, and what do you know . . . there was Naomi, again. I nearly walked right into her. Looking back, we were clearly destined. At the time, I was just glad to see someone who could point me in the right direction. "Hey, Naomi!" I said. "How do I get to Covent Garden?"

"We're going that way. Come walk with us," she said, so I joined the girls for the ten-minute walk to the restaurant. Three random encounters in one night? It was fate. And there you have it.

Ibiza Sant Josep de sa Talaia 07817

The British were much further ahead than Americans early in the new century in terms of texting; it was the latest craze there. It turned out that Naomi's company used an early version of the cell phones that texted messages—something new and different to me at that time. I spent the next couple of weeks busily settling legal matters and rehearsing for opening night, but Naomi and I communicated by phone several times a day. It was fun, and a good way to get to know her better, with no pressure. By the time I got around to actually inviting her to see the show, I felt that I already knew her.

Naomi came backstage after the performance and we went out to dinner afterward. The restaurant was amazing and we drank a fantastic bottle of wine. We completely closed the bar down at four A.M. because we had so much to talk about. It was the best date of my life . . . only ending the next morning because Naomi had to scramble to get to her job! I was crazy about this girl. I planned something special for our second date: a whirlwind trip to Paris for the weekend. She was that special, and I wanted her to know I knew it.

From that point on, we were inseparable. Naomi would come to meet me after every show and we'd go out. In a happy coincidence, my old friend Stephanie Beacham was appearing in *A Fine Day* at the theater next door to ours. There was something special about the way my career had circled back to being so near to her again. I was an adult this time. Stephanie was as beautiful as ever, with a young and gorgeous boyfriend not yet out of his twenties. The four of us spent many evenings together over long dinners and she would watch enviously as Naomi and I drank whiskey. "I remember when I could drink whiskey," she'd say, sighing. "Now I get too hungover."

Sometimes Naomi and I would just go to my place and cook and listen to music, stay up late and talk . . . whatever we did together, I was happy.

Although our romance was going great, Naomi's job was not. I was keeping her up far too late every night. After a certain point, she became so sleep deprived that she started falling asleep on the job. I was on a theater schedule while Naomi had a regular office job, and those hours did not mesh. Naomi created a small sleeping area under her desk that she used to crawl into and nap for brief periods of time each day. She reasoned that she was only taking the same amount of the time the smokers in the office did for breaks. Her supervisor did not see it that way, and she was given an official warning, but it didn't slow either of us down.

On Sundays we had picnics, played Frisbee in Hyde Park, or watched the old noir movies that I loved . . . it was a perfect romance. I was in no hurry to leave London. Conveniently, the play kept going and going. *Side Man* had originally been a three-month engagement, but it turned into six months. Eventually, it was time to go and it was horrible to say good-bye to Naomi, but I knew it wouldn't be for long.

Naomi had a long-planned holiday with a group of her college friends coming up in the summer on the island of Ibiza. When she told me of her plans, I said, "Great, I've always wanted to go to Ibiza— I'll meet you there!" Naomi was quite taken aback by the very forward Americanness of this—no proper British boyfriend would ever presume to join someone's vacation—even if it was his own girlfriend. I was definitely shaking this girl's life up!

I finished the play and returned to New York, diving back into the nightlife for a month. My sister flew in from L.A. and met me, and the two of us were off to Ibiza so that we could meet and spend a week together, just the two of us. Then Naomi would arrive, and the three of us would have a week together. The following week, all of Naomi's friends would arrive, and we would all hang out together. That was the plan.

There is no way to describe what a magical place Ibiza is, and what a crazy vacation it was. Lying just off the coast of Spain in the middle of the Mediterranean Sea, the tiny island has a very well deserved international reputation for nightlife. In the twenty-one days I spent there, I probably saw twenty sunrises. We would all go dancing at one of the huge clubs where the roof rolled back at dawn and hundreds of revelers from every corner of the globe would all burst into cheers and applause at the sight of another day in paradise.

There was amazing food, ridiculous amounts of alcohol, numerous illegal substances, naps, swimming, sand, sun, friends, naked cliff diving . . . you name it, we did it. It was the wildest, most uninhibited vacation of my life and one that could never happen today. Thank God there was no YouTube or camera phones back then! Suffice it to say, we all let loose on the ultimate vacation. And the best part about it was that Naomi and I fell more in love by the day.

Stockholm
SE-106 91

I didn't see any reason to slow the party down, so I decided, on a whim, to attend the MTV Music Video Awards in Stockholm that fall. As I was checking into my hotel, someone tackled me from behind and I wound up sprawled flat on the floor in front of the check-in desk. I leaped up, fists in the air, ready for a fight. Larry Mullen, the drummer from U2, was standing there laughing at me. This was his welcome. "Jason! Can't believe you're here! We're in the bar, man; come along now, join us!" he said, in his thick Irish accent.

I literally just tossed my bag toward the front desk and accompanied Larry into the bar, where the party was well under way. Larry, Bono, the Edge, and I had a few drinks, then we all headed out into Stockholm. Now Bono is a guy about my size, about five foot eight or nine, average height. In Stockholm, every single person over the age of twelve, male or female, is blond, beautiful, and six feet plus.

Bono and I stood in the corner of the most happening nightclub in the city and with beers in hand took in the scene and all the unbelievably gorgeous girls. After a few minutes, he turned to me and said, "Jason, I've never felt so short and unattractive in me life." Eventually, we returned to the hotel bar. Robbie Williams was there with his manager, and the two were engaged in a very heated argument. Suddenly, Robbie turned and just decked his manager, who fell unconscious in a heap on the floor. It was complete mayhem. But what did I expect, hanging out with U2?

The next year I found myself in Indianapolis doing color commentary for the Indy 500. U2 was coming to town for a concert, which happened to fall on Bono's birthday. Of course it had been sold out forever. I called their manager and said, "Paul, hey I'm here in town. Any way I can get a ticket to the show?"

"Sure, no problem about the ticket, Jason, but I just don't know what's happening after the show. I think the guys are planning to finish the gig, race to the airport, and take off for New York City immediately."

"Oh, no, of course, I really would just love to see the show." When I got to the stadium, I didn't have a seat. I sat at the mixing board instead with the sound guy, where the view and the sound were absolutely incredible, and watched the opening act, British singer PJ Harvey. I was already a big fan of her work, so I was excited to see her perform. Then U2 came on and blew the place away. I was immediately and completely lost in their music.

Except somebody kept jostling me. I tried to ignore it but finally turned around, and there was PJ Harvey herself with a bottle of champagne in her hand. I stuck out my hand and introduced myself, telling her what a big fan I was of her music. Next thing I knew I was having a glass of champagne with PJ, watching the U2 concert from the mixing board. It was great to be me that night.

Echo Park
90026

Because of my DUI case, I still had no driver's license, so when I got an invitation to Jennie Garth's wedding, I flew to L.A. and had to take a limo to the ceremony in Santa Barbara. This was the first time I'd seen everybody since I'd left the show, so it was a minireunion of sorts for me.

Jennie was finally making it official with her longtime boyfriend, the actor Peter Facinelli. He'd been around forever. She and Peter got married at Our Lady of Mount Carmel Church in a Catholic ceremony. Their adorable toddler daughter, Luca Bella, was the flower girl; Tori and Tiffani served as bridesmaids, and I had a fine time catching up with everyone at the reception. I spent most of my time hanging out with Ian, whose company I always enjoyed, and his first wife, Nikki, along with Tiff and her boyfriend, Brady. All my old cast mates were settling down, starting families, and getting on with life after the show.

The lavish reception was held at the Bacara Resort, one of the most gorgeous locations on the Santa Barbara coast and after an evening of partying, everyone stayed overnight. The next morning I got into a town car to take care of one more piece of business. I knew I sure as hell wasn't headed anywhere resembling the Bacara. I was off to Los Angeles to serve my DUI time at a minimum-security federal facility.

For my DUI offense, I was sentenced to spend five nights in a halfway house. The home was located in Echo Park, an east L.A.

neighborhood bisected by Sunset Boulevard that has, in recent years, become trendy and revitalized but at the time was still quite rough. This was not a prison as it was located on residential property, but even so, I won't lie; it was scary walking through that door. I had never been in trouble with the law before, and now I was heading into a place where all my freedom would be taken away. Not to mention all my stuff! Wallet, ID, keys, phone—everything had to be handed over. I certainly hadn't realized how attached I was to my personal possessions until everything was taken away and tagged, bagged, and stored. At least I got to wear my own clothes.

The staffer who had checked me in and taken all my property led me out of the intake building into a yard. Not a prison yard, just a shabby suburban backyard covered in dead brown grass and cracked concrete patios. We walked to one of several nondescript bungalows and went inside. The place was split into two small bedrooms and a tiny bathroom. I threw the bag of toiletries they had provided down on what the counselor told me was my bunk and headed back outside.

All my fellow "inmates" were sitting around a large beat-up picnic table playing some sort of game that involved a great deal of gesturing, screaming, and dramatic tearing up and throwing of cards. All the talk was in Russian. I had no idea what the hell was going on, but knew I had to break the ice sometime. I approached the table warily as the group of hard-faced men stopped their game and watched me in silence. Suddenly, the biggest guy at the table—who was straight out of central casting as a mob boss—jumped up and strode toward me. I braced myself. Then: "Brrran-don!" he said, with a thick Russian accent, and picked me up off the ground in a bear hug.

I think I'm going to be okay in here, I thought with relief.

I plunked myself down in the middle of the group and watched the action. My fellow players were all Russian, serving time for what I would call various "white collar" offenses. There was definitely a large Russian mob presence in Los Angeles, but these apparently weren't the real hard cases. These guys had been convicted of various types of schemes: they were tax dodgers or had committed medical insurance fraud or some other type of corporate malfeasance. My roommate was in for some kind of former "prescription drug" something or other—I didn't understand and didn't particularly care to know the details.

I tried to play their crazy card game for the next five days, but never quite grasped the complicated rules. I also entertained the group with stories of life on *90210*. The middle-aged Russians were riveted! I must admit, they were all pretty cool guys, and I didn't have so much a scary time as a strange, slightly surreal, and, let's face it, boring one. Look, clearly the place wasn't Oz, but it wasn't fun. I never, ever wanted to go back.

My time was served, the deal was done, and my driver's license was restored. I had taken my eyes off the prize and deserved every bit of my punishment. Not to get all kumbaya about it, but the results were clear when I had no structure, no plans, and no goals. This is what resulted—nothing good. I vowed it would not happen again.

Ray Art Studios
Canoga Park
91304

Shannen Doherty was lucky enough to have lightning strike twice in her career—both times with Aaron Spelling. After finalizing all my legal matters, I set up a few meetings. One day, I headed to a studio deep in the Valley to see a producer. As I walked into the studio, I saw they were shooting *Charmed,* so I wandered over and saw my old friend Betty Reardon, a producer from *90210,* who now worked there.

"Betty, wow, what's been going on?" We caught up and she said, "Hey, Shannen's here today, you've got to go see her!"

I headed back toward the trailers and found hers. I banged on the door and after she opened it, I grabbed her and gave her a big hug. She was very surprised to see me. "Come in, sit down, talk to me!" she said. "What is going on?"

"Shannen, I am so happy for you," I told her sincerely. "The show is great, a big hit, and you're doing so well. This is awesome. But seriously, girl, how did you talk Aaron into giving you another show? Tell me!"

I wasn't even kidding. I really wanted to know.

Shannen launched into an explanation. She told me that she'd heard about the script, gotten her hands on a copy, and read it. She knew right away that she could bring something special to the role of Prue, the bravest and most powerful sister, and somehow felt personally drawn to this show. It offered her the perfect opportunity to spin all her previous bad press into something new and Aaron had agreed.

"Shannen, that's genius," I told her, in all sincerity. I was pleased to see her doing so well.

However, within five minutes she was already complaining about Alyssa Milano and how she didn't want to work with her, and that she was going to call Aaron, and he would have to make a choice—"her or me," as she put it. I couldn't believe what I was hearing.

"Shannen, what the hell? Don't do that! Do you understand how lucky you are to have an opportunity like this, a great role on another hit show? Why would you do anything to screw this up for yourself? Come in every morning, know your lines, hit your marks, and keep your mouth shut! Don't make waves; just be cool and make it work!"

"But, Jason, you don't understand . . ." and off she went for a good twenty minutes. I listened, and then tried again. Eventually, I was sure I'd made my point and that what I was saying had sunk in.

It was not to be. By the end of the season, Shannen was off another hit Spelling television show.

Tribeca
10013

In March of 2001, I asked Naomi to officially come live with me in New York, and she accepted. The two of us loved it there, and we had a fantastic time. We were two young people in love, living in a fantastic loft in Tribeca, with plenty of time and money . . . kids in a candy store. What's not to like about that city? Believe me, we took a big bite out of that apple. Restaurants, nightlife, parties, shopping, shows—we did it all, every day and night, then did it all over again the next day.

The only one not happy was my beloved dog, Swifty, who did not care for life in New York. He would very begrudgingly go outside, do his business on the sidewalk, then turn around, ready to go back in. He hated the noise, the honking, the crowds, the heat in summer, the cold in winter. He didn't even like going to the dog park to play with other dogs! This West Coast dog would have none of it. He preferred hanging out in the loft, lying on the sofa sleeping, or watching television. He was a funny little guy, but always great company.

Naomi, with her degree in fine art from Nottingham Trent University, found a job at an art gallery. She began selling lots of pieces to all kinds of crazy-rich people on the fringes of the art world, and we soon fell in with a group of "trustafarian" kids who literally had more money than they could ever spend and nothing but free time to run all over the city and do whatever they wanted. These guys—and girls—

had no limits. I never once saw an off switch. It was New York—go go go go go go—and for a while it was superfun.

My buddy the hockey star Theo Fleury had signed a four-year, 32-million-dollar contract with the New York Rangers and bought a place outside the city up in Rye. Theo had a lovely wife, Veronica, and two small kids, so they were considerably calmer than the crowd we'd been seeing. Naomi and I started spending time with the Fleurys as they were a bit more in tune with what we were looking to do in the future, and I was more than happy to be around another Canadian again!

At a certain point we could no longer keep up with the trustafarians; we just didn't have their stamina. I was far from old, and Naomi was the same age as they were, but we were the ones who simply had to call it a night at some ridiculous hour, while they were just getting going. Seriously, the party never stopped . . . they may possibly have been the hardest-partying group of people I ever partied with, which is certainly saying something (#CharlieSheen#RobertDowneyJunior). These were brief, intense, but transitory friendships where we hung out all the time and then everybody moved on. That's the joy of New York City.

Instead, we began to spend more and more time at Madison Square Garden and got very into the hockey scene, socializing with the Rangers crowd, which was incredibly fun for me. Being around that whole organization was fantastic. Theo and Veronica were definitely not "trustafarians," but we all certainly managed to have fun in the city. Maybe too much fun. Theo's ongoing struggles with drugs and alcohol had been well documented, and I witnessed a few worrisome incidents that I couldn't ignore. It was no longer all fun and games and there were some serious consequences for my amazingly talented but troubled friend. Eventually, I was forced to take a good look at myself as well.

New York was dangerous. It didn't seem so at the time, of course. I was navigating some tricky waters as a young man who was young and successful, had worked his ass off, and now wanted to have some fun. The opportunities were constantly there with drugs. My life had started to spiral downward a little—slowly, imperceptibly, but going down all the same . . . and had been for a while. For the first time in years, I had plenty of time on my hands, and I never did well without lots of balls in the air. For a long time I'd forgotten that, as I felt that my more relaxed lifestyle was well deserved after a decade of hard work.

I wasn't working much at the time, so there were no more 6:30 set calls in the mornings. I'd lost my ride, not having driven race cars since MCI had gone under. I was a young guy with money and a great girlfriend. It was party time—until I could no longer deny that it was heading to a place I most definitely did not want to go. In the past, I had always been able to snap back to my professional self when there was work to do—I never fooled around with work, ever.

Still, I wasn't doing anything productive with my days. In fact, I was sleeping away plenty of my days because my nights were so active. I was pretty aimless, and that was not good. I liked to have purpose, a reason to jump out of bed every morning. I thrive on goal setting and structure. I had no goals besides having a good time; conversely, everything that had kept me in line in the past was no longer there.

Having Naomi live with me was a huge move, one that in retrospect I am not sure either one of us really thought through completely. We hadn't taken into account the kind of strain it would cause for her to move to a new city where she didn't know anybody. We were no longer courting in London; she wasn't visiting for five days; this was now her permanent life. We were both settling into a regular daily pattern. The novelty of life in a new country wore off for her, and the adjustment was tough. On both of us.

I was pushing the recreational habit hard—drinking, smoking cigarettes, and becoming irresponsible in a number of ways that were just not me. Skipping commitments here and there . . . being late . . . not returning calls . . . not being where I said I'd be . . . blowing friends off. At the time I felt these were all small things, and for a long time I found them easy to justify. It was insidious, actually. But I'm not the kind of guy who can kid himself for long. I realized pretty fast that I was going to do permanent damage to my relationship with Naomi, not to mention my career and reputation, which I had spent so many years creating and building. I hadn't blown anything up yet, but this messing around had to stop. It was a humbling realization.

It was a hard pill to swallow, if you'll excuse the expression. It's always difficult to admit you're wrong, admit you're weak, admit there's something you can't handle—that you've made a mistake. I had been taking care of myself and making my own decisions since I was seventeen years old, and most had turned out well. It hurt my pride to admit failure and defeat. But make no mistake about it, my excessive partying had to stop.

All the goals that I had set for myself as a young man, I had attained. And I hadn't bothered to set new ones. That was a big mistake. But one that I would rectify.

Indianapolis Motor Speedway 46222

I had no ride but wanted to stay involved in the racing world, so when I got a call from the Indy Racing League, I listened to their offer. Buddy McAtee asked if I wanted to meet with Bob Goodrich at NBC and talk about doing some color commentating for the IRL. I met with Bob and we explored the possibilities, and then ABC offered me the job. At that time in 2001, another Hollywood writers' strike was looming, which was supposed to cripple the industry and bring show business to a screeching halt. I remembered the last strike, so when I got this offer, I figured why not? I should stay busy. How long could it take, anyway? Fourteen races? No big deal.

So . . . I joined the team and became a color commentator. I am here to say that while it was fun, and an excellent learning experience, I had absolutely no idea of everything that went into being a color commentator, or any sort of broadcaster. I had never done anything like that in my life, and it was much more difficult than I could have anticipated. I have a tremendous amount of respect for all those guys, as that was one tough job. I sat in the booth with well-known broadcasters Bob Jenkins and Larry Rice, while Jack Arute and Vince Welsh were the pit guys, giving viewers' reports from the pits.

The entire time I was broadcasting two guys were talking to me, one in each ear, giving constant updates and information and direction. Meanwhile, I had to process what the other hosts were saying, while following the action and holding up my end of the commentary. When you're a pro, it all looks and sounds very natural; trust me, it's not. It's a hard freaking job!

By far the best part of the whole experience was getting to call the Indy 500 with the legendary Al Michaels. As much fun as I had that year, however, it was indisputable that I was not a broadcaster . . . nor did I want to be. The memories were priceless, and I was glad I did it, but I was relieved when the season ended and I could return to my regular job. Of course, the writers' strike that everyone had been fearing never actually materialized, so I really should have been working instead of broadcasting. However, I would never walk out on a commitment, and being allowed to sit in the booth, calling races, will remain a very cool memory for my entire life.

Best of all, since I was hanging around the paddock that whole year, when the IRL was thinking of bringing the Indy Lights racing series back, they thought of me. Kelley Racing called and asked me to campaign a car for them in what would now be called the Infiniti Pro Series. The series was being rebranded to highlight Infiniti, their big engine sponsor.

Now this was my kind of racing offer—a fantastic opportunity. Of course I agreed!

Outpost Estates
Hollywood Hills
90068

Excited about my new racing opportunities, I had nearly six months to fill before race season started so I returned to Toronto to do a couple of quick movies for my friend Peter Simpson. Then, while working on these short projects, I wound up signing to do a few more quickies. I was spending so much time there that I finally just bought a condo and lived in Toronto for six straight months.

While staying in Toronto with me, Naomi decided to pursue a dream she'd been nurturing for quite some time—to study to become a professional makeup artist. Since her teenage years she had been fascinated with cosmetics; she was the girl who always loved making up her friend's faces. What she really wanted to do was learn how to do special effects makeup, a very complicated art. It was a natural profession for her, given her interest in arts and painting and sculpting. She took advantage of my time parked in Toronto and enrolled in the Makeup School. She was completely occupied with her classes the entire time we were there and got officially certified—first in her class!—just as it was time to head back to New York.

As my film projects were wrapping up, I made a quick trip to Los Angeles for several meetings. I met with Anthony Edwards at his production company on the Paramount lot and read for Tony and his partner, Dante Di Loreto (later to be the big-time television producer of *Glee*). I was going for a part in their new film *Die Mommie Die!*, starring Charles Busch and Natasha Lyonne, along with a very interesting group of performers. I landed the role and was asked to return to L.A. in June 2002 to begin shooting.

I also had a meeting with my agent, who pointed out that I'd been in New York for quite a while. "It's probably time for you to return to L.A. You've been gone for so long, everyone has pretty much forgotten what you look like." I had to agree. I thought that I should probably start looking around at houses. I put the Tribeca condo on the market and called my friend Fred Henry, a real estate broker in L.A.

Fred took me to see a few properties and we looked at a 1928 Spanish home in the Hollywood Hills that was just right. The house was in a very desirable neighborhood called Outpost Estates, a hillside community of 450 '20s-style homes. The area was popular with actors and entertainment industry people, and I'd often dreamed of owning a house there someday. Built into the hill, the home's garage was on the street level, with fifty-two steps leading up to the front door. I put in an offer immediately.

Production on *Die Mommie Die!* turned out to be an unbelievable experience and resulted in a campy, funny cult classic. I was in L.A. shooting the movie for the month of June and began the racing season for Kelley, then raced back to Toronto as soon as production wrapped. I helped Naomi sell a bunch of stuff, then we packed up the few things that were left and shipped them to our new home in L.A. Our good furniture and everything else we owned was still in the New York condo, which we were showing furnished to attract prospective buyers. We didn't have anything for the new house and we pretty much walked in the door to our new home that July with only two suitcases.

By this time, I was halfway through the racing season, driving the Kelley racing entry in the Infiniti Pro Series, and everything was going quite well; I was in third place overall and had been consistently running up front. I had to fly east for a race, so I looked around the empty house and told Naomi, "I'm just going to this race in Kentucky. When I get back, hopefully everything we shipped should be here, and we'll deal with this empty house. See you on Sunday night, after the race."

Kentucky Speedway
41806

The air was heavy and damp on that humid day in the middle of summer 2002 in the South. At the halfway point in the official season, I was third in line for the championship. I was driving my Infiniti Pro Series car, which is basically a 200 mph open wheel oval car, for the Kelley Racing Team. It looked like an Indy car but was a little bit smaller and a little bit slower.

We drivers took our regular warm-up laps, very standard, when somebody blew an engine. As usual, workers ran out and put down something called Quick Dry on the track. It soaked up all the oils and antifreeze and fluids. Usually, it zapped any moisture and blew away in an instant. Because of the weather that day, the Quick Dry didn't blow away immediately.

Practice time was almost over; I'm not sure why they even sent us back out for more laps. Still, we returned to the track, and as I was coming out of turn one, a wheel touched the Quick Dry. I mean, barely touched it, and boom, I was in the wall at 187 miles an hour. It was over in an instant. The curtain came down, and I woke up three weeks later.

Although I was awake and talking during much of the next twenty days, I have absolutely no memory of it. Three weeks of my life were gone, and I will never get them back. Of course, I certainly heard plenty about them from friends and family.

AFTER THE WRECK, I was airlifted to the University of Kentucky Medical Center to be stabilized. I was bleeding out so fast that medical staff met the helicopter on the roof of the hospital with bags of O negative and immediately made transfusions to keep me alive. The seat belt that crossed my neck had sliced my carotid artery, so I was blowing blood seven feet in the air. There was a real danger of me bleeding to death before they could get me inside.

Jim Freudenberg, the Kelley Racing team manager, called my father in Canada from the hospital and said, "You need to get here, now." He hung up and made the same call to Naomi, who was unpacking boxes in our new house. They were freaking out; the first reports on the news erroneously stated that I had died, causing a media sensation. My mother had seen my death announced on a news crawl across the television as she sipped her morning coffee and was devastated as she frantically called my sister in New York. There was general panic among my family members as they all scrambled to catch flights from their various locations.

The two days were incredibly tense as doctors and nurses worked around the clock to stabilize me. As the staff worked heroically on me, there were two moments when I died on the table. Literally, flatlined. There was some concern I would have to have excess fluid drained from my brain, but fortunately that turned out to be unnecessary. A tube was installed to drain excess fluid from my lungs. I had a separate oxygen tube down my throat at all times to sustain me. Unconscious and with a broken back, I was fed intravenously from a bag of white goo packed full of nutrients to keep me alive.

Naomi, carrying Swifty, had been the first to arrive on a flight from Los Angeles. She was horrified when I emerged from intensive care. My eyes were protruding like tennis balls, and my nose was literally ripped off my face. They had pulled it back and tacked it down temporarily, but it looked monstrous. She tiptoed around to sit at my bedside, gently holding my hand and saying my name. I didn't stir.

Luke Perry happened to be working in Nashville when the news broke about my accident. He was the next to arrive. When Luke came in my room, he got right in my face and said, "Who am I? What's my name?" Everyone waited for a response. "Who am I? What's my name?" he repeated a little louder this time. I finally responded. "Coy L. Perry," I whispered. My throat was dry and had been damaged by the breathing tube they had used to resuscitate me.

The doctors and nurses all looked confused, until Luke informed them that Coy was indeed his name . . . his real name. . . .

They then all looked more than a little relieved, as this was more brain function than I had shown in the previous two days. I was starting to show signs of stabilizing. It wouldn't be long before I would be moving on to the doctors who would be tasked with putting my broken body back together.

Rehabilitation Hospital of Indiana 46254

I was unloaded from another helicopter, once again put in intensive care, and prepped for back surgery. Dr. Terry Trammell, renowned surgeon and now retired, was probably the best in the world at putting race car drivers back together again. He was a genius, and he's the one who undertook the delicate operation to put my spine back together. Two rods plus twelve screws in the back; the surgery was absolutely brutal. It was also quite dangerous, as he had cautioned my father and Naomi beforehand. There were no guarantees but, fortunately, it was determined that I had come through with flying colors—no paralysis. I was one of the lucky ones.

Very shortly after the surgery, I woke up in the middle of the night, calling for Naomi. She and my sister, Justine, rushed to my side to ask how I felt. I looked at them and said very clearly, "I saw the devil." "And what happened?" they asked. "I embraced him," I said. "Then I pushed him away." The words were so eerie and cryptic from someone who had pretty much awoken from the dead that they completely freaked out. They called the doctors and wrote down the phrase to ask me about later; but it was my deep unconscious responding.

After ten days in the hospital, I was moved to the Rehabilitation Hospital of Indiana. RHI is the phenomenal facility where I was faced with major rehab. They have many of the finest surgeons and physical therapists in the world on staff. At some point after my arrival, I woke up one day and asked where I was. Naomi patiently explained where I was and what had happened to me, for probably the tenth time. I'd asked and been told the details many times and had held full conversations with several people. However, I hadn't been present for those. This time I was really awake for good. I was back from dreamland, and I was one hurting guy.

I was on some major heavy-duty painkillers, and I could feel them slowing down my mind. A few days later I called Dr. Scheid and Dr. Trammell to my bedside and said to them, "I am on so many drugs, guys, I don't know how I'm really doing. I've got to get off all these painkillers."

"That's not a good idea, Jason," they said.

"Just take me off everything . . . and then we can establish a baseline of exactly where I'm at. I'm not even sure what really hurts!" I said. Somehow, I talked them into it, and the drugs were slowly withdrawn over the next four hours. Once they were out of my system, I wanted them back. Quick! That was a very uncomfortable hour, particularly for my back. My feet, though wrecked, were completely bound up in casts, so that wasn't the worst, but my back—the pain was excruciating.

I was sweating and in complete agony when they resumed painkillers, though at a greatly reduced dose. They slapped a transdermal patch on me, and in a few minutes the relief flooded through my body. I had established a baseline all right! It hurt like hell! My brain was still scrambled from the concussion, but now it wasn't also clouded by so many drugs. I felt much better on lower doses. I was ready to start the healing process.

The day of my accident had been a bad day all round for the Kelley Racing Team. One of the guys from our team got run over in the pits, broke his pelvis, and wound up in the same rehab facility as I did. As I got stronger, I used to laboriously get out of bed, get myself situated in my wheelchair, and roll over to visit him, to see how he was doing and talk about racing.

I was highly motivated and trying hard to get out of the hospital. My day was filled to the brim. I'd wake up in the morning and have breakfast. Then a physical therapist would come and we'd head to the gym for exercises and therapy. Next I had speech therapy, which I very much needed. I couldn't speak clearly; in fact, I was slurring my words like the victim of a minor stroke. Patiently, laboriously, we worked on my speech and pronunciation every day.

In the afternoons, I had intensive cognitive therapy. My therapist would ask me to remember three words—say, *cat, hat,* and *red.* Then we would speak for two minutes. When the two minutes were up, she would say, "What are the three words I asked you to remember?" Try as I might, for a good while I could not even recall one of them. She spent a great deal of time encouraging me, explaining how my brain was capable of amazing feats. It would remap itself. My brain would search out and find new routes to take to bypass the damaged parts. I needed to read, and do logic problems, and play memorization games, but besides that, all I could do was wait and let my brain heal.

I had never been much good at waiting. I had a heart-to-heart one day with Dr. Trammell. "What kind of healing process should I be expecting?" I asked him.

"If you stop smoking right now, your spine—and the other bones—will heal in one year. Your bones should be as hard and sturdy as they were before the accident. If you resume smoking when you leave the hospital, you can expect the entire healing cycle to take three years—oh, and your bones will never be the same."

"Guess I just quit smoking," I told him. Actually, I had "quit" the moment I hit the wall. I never started again. I was an actor in the 1990s so of course I smoked, we all did. But I never picked up another butt. It just wasn't worth it. Hell, I'd already died twice now, and coming back to life wasn't much fun.

Thank God Naomi and I were both young and somewhat naive; she never doubted I would make a full recovery. After a few dark nights of the soul, neither did I. I swore to myself that I would return to 100 percent of what I had been before the accident. Knowing me so well and how to best motivate me, Naomi was behind me the whole way, encouraging and pushing when needed. "Come on now, get with it, let's go," she would say in my rare moments of balking. It wasn't whether or not I would get better, but when.

My cognitive therapist was simply fantastic, though I have to say everybody on staff at RHI was amazing. As I improved, she got her hands on some scripts and read scenes with me every day. She was looking ahead, helping me relearn how to memorize dialogue, so I could hopefully resume my regular life and job one day. It was looking a bit more hopeful as the weeks passed.

Jim and Cindy's House
Indianapolis
46251

After a month of living at RHI, Naomi and I moved into my team manager's home. Jim and his wife, Cindy, put us up in Indianapolis while I continued my rehab. It was a tremendous relief to be out of the hospital setting and the discharge did wonders for my mood. I was still back and forth every day to RHI for physical therapy, but the simple pleasure of actually living in a house again was amazing. Jim was absolutely great, every frustrating step of the way. He was rock solid the entire time of my recovery. A true friend.

I had plenty of time to ponder during this time. My overriding feeling the first few months after the accident was surprise. Like all race car drivers, I honestly never dreamed I could get hurt racing. Oh, I'd had some minor injuries here and there . . . but in a million years I wouldn't have imagined this could happen to me. I felt safer in a race car than I did in my regular car driving home from the track. One minute I was a thirty-two-year-old race car driver, happy as can be, and the next, I was . . . dead, and then slowly brought back to life again. I had just . . . never . . . thought.

Still, there must have been something tiny nagging at the back of my mind going into that season. Running the Infiniti Pro series, I had known I was going to be racing on ovals. Oval racing is inherently more dangerous than any other kind, and of course I was aware of that. For the first time in my life, I had bought extra supplemental race car driver insurance. In all my previous years of driving, I had never felt the need for it. For whatever reason, that year I bought the extra policy. Thank God I did. Needless to say, the hospital bills were staggering. Much later, going through the bills, we were shocked to see my daily bag of food, the white goo, cost a thousand dollars a day!

I was not allowed to leave until the screws were taken out of my feet. Man, did they hurt when those came out! I was limping, skinny, and weak. But I had my dog and my girl by my side. It was not quite the return to L.A. my agents and I had envisioned, but we were coming home.

My wreck and recovery were big news in the entertainment and racing media, and I was deluged with interview requests once I was out of the hospital and throughout my recovery. "How did this experience change you?" was the main question from reporters. I usually answered that it hadn't, because on the outside nothing had changed. Thankfully, my body was healing, and I looked the same on the outside. I didn't drive any more slowly, I wasn't any more careful, I would absolutely consider racing again . . . outwardly, to the public eye, nothing had changed. Internally, everything had.

One very painful aspect of the accident to me was some subtle and not-so-subtle references in the press to my "party" reputation, my DUI charge, and speculations about what, exactly, had caused me to wreck . . . a hangover, maybe? That was ridiculous, not to mention ironic, as I had never been as stone-cold sober as I was in my current lifestyle. The accident caused another seismic shift inside me, in the overall way I looked at life.

I'd always been able to set a goal, work hard, attain it. Set another goal, work even harder, attain it. That was how I'd lived my entire life and it had worked out well so far, including the decision to cool it on my brief indolent party lifestyle. But I had returned right away to my old habits of constantly striving to achieve. Apart from that one brief period, I was again a hamster on a wheel, running as fast as I could, never taking any time to stop and look around and actually enjoy the amazing experiences I was having, appreciating the fruits of my labor, or anything else. I didn't spend any real quality time with the people I loved. I was always so focused on attaining the next goal that life was passing me by.

Looking in the mirror, I realized that I was no longer the boy I had been. At thirty-three years old, I needed to become the man I wanted to be. It was an incredibly powerful wake-up call and growing experience. This was my biggest challenge ever: to put myself back together physically and mentally and come out better and stronger on the other end. I had to relearn how to talk and think and move. My memory was shot. The recovery process would be grueling and painful, and I had to push myself like never before.

During the couple of years leading up to the accident, I'd been searching for something that I couldn't find. Professionally, I was somewhat adrift, feeling a little disenfranchised from the industry. Personally, I had one piece of the puzzle: a beautiful woman and true partner at my side. She was both my equal in many ways and my better half. We shared the same diverse interests, and she was a rock during my recovery.

The accident reset me immediately on my career goals and how to get the life I wanted and needed. There was an immediate change in my attitude and the way that I conducted myself. I became far more protective of my time, my relationship with Naomi, plans made with family and friends. I began to consider the future and what kind of legacy I wanted to leave—and I wanted it to be more than "starring in a classic American television show." I had been granted another chance at life, and I wasn't about to waste it.

Outpost Estates 90068

Twelve weeks after the date of my accident, I was finally allowed to return to Los Angeles. Naomi, Swifty, and I arrived at our empty new house in the hills, vastly relieved to be home. I was battered, but alive, and all in one piece. Time to face the steep hillside and the fifty-two steps that led to the front door. I hadn't given them a thought when I bought the house, thinking they were beautiful and quaint. Naomi and I were both young and in great shape then. Now . . . not so much. In and out, every time I left the house . . . fifty-two steps down and fifty-two back up on my poor battered feet. I cursed those steps every day, under my breath, as I stopped to rest halfway.

I was well enough to live at home, but my body was still very messed up. All the determination in the world couldn't make me better faster. It was going to take time to heal; I was still quite broken and damaged. Still, I had my task set and was feeling completely un-daunted now that I was free. My goal was to be 100 percent exactly as I had been before, both physically and mentally, within one year of the accident. I absolutely refused to allow one racing incident, from the sport I loved so much, keep me from getting on with my life. That accident would not impede my future in any way. I simply wouldn't allow it.

I woke up every morning, ate breakfast, and then headed to the gym for what had once been my regular routine. I had to slowly ease back into it, because I had absolutely no muscle mass. It had vanished over the weeks of lying in bed. I was thin and weak, and I knew it would take time and patience to rebuild my body. My gym routine took a couple of hours every day.

When I came home, I would leaf through one of the many cookbooks in the house and settle on one of the most complicated, involved recipes I could find. I only chose dishes that before the accident I simply had not had the time to tackle. I now had nothing but time on my hands. I was free to spend all day preparing coq au vin or cassoulet. My entire challenge for every afternoon was to make dinner. Trust me: at the time, creating these dinners was always a four- or five-hour ordeal.

I mixed and measured, sliced, chopped, and pureed. The math involved in measuring ingredients or adapting recipes gave my brain a good workout. Cooking is all about timing and multitasking. It was not easy, and there were some major mishaps along the way, but my reward was usually a delicious dinner. Meal preparation became a huge part of my rehabilitation and something that carried on well after my recovery. To this very day, when I'm home, I'm the cook.

I put any thoughts of work on the back burner. I was in no condition to do anything more than I was doing, and even I knew it. Four months after the wreck, Naomi and I spent our first Christmas together at our house in the Hollywood Hills. I was starting to look and feel like my old self again. My strength was returning. The pain was lessening every day. We toasted the New Year with great optimism.

I WAS SPENDING all my afternoons in our big old kitchen with the original 1928 cabinetry—though it had a modern range and refrigerator. It was such a fantastic room, the best place in the house. Naomi and I both loved cooking or just hanging out in there.

One day we made roasted garlic meatballs, a phenomenal recipe but ridiculously complicated and time-consuming. Somehow, we didn't realize that we would wind up with thirty-six meatballs. We were faced with this ridiculously huge mound of meatballs. "Crap, honey, what are we going to do with all this freaking food?" I asked her.

"I know!" Naomi said. "I'll run over and ask the neighbors if they'd like to have dinner with us." Jack and Dennis were partners, in work and in life; we'd spoken briefly to them out on the street the day we moved in. I thought inviting them was a great idea so we both put on our shoes, went down the fifty-two steps, and crossed the street to knock on our neighbors' door.

"Hi, guys! We made way too much food. Can you come over and help us eat it?" Our neighbors accepted and showed up a few minutes later. I headed to the wine cellar and started pulling corks, and dinner with our new friends began. It turned into an unbelievable five-hour-long feast, and they literally rolled themselves home. (It wasn't until years later that they told us they had already eaten a big meal that night, but wanted to connect, so they came over for dinner anyway and stuffed down some meatballs.)

After that we saw them frequently—generally starting around happy hour. I'd get a cheese plate and pâté going, and they would drop by after work. Our neighbors were quite successful. They owned a construction company and did renovations on high-end homes. Jack was in charge of the design, and Dennis did the construction. Eventually, they were showing up nearly every day to drink wine and chat. It became the norm . . . no one had any kids, I wasn't working, the company did me good, and I had a very appreciative audience for my meals and wine.

One evening, Dennis fell down the steps in front of the house, which were quite old and narrow. Quite a lot of wine had been drunk, and down those fifty-two steps he tumbled. Fortunately, he wasn't hurt, and because they were real friends, they didn't sue. After that we installed a handrail for our tipsy "gaybors," as we wanted them to get home safely every night!

We are great friends to this day, though no longer neighbors. It was a bit of a blow to them when we moved; certainly no one else was serving Château Lafite at happy hour!

Baffin Island
Iqaluit
XOA OHO

By the time spring arrived in 2003, six or seven months after my accident, I was getting restless. I kept up my gym routine and was doing well. Mentally and physically, I was feeling pretty good. It crossed my mind that I could probably return to work. A couple of days later, as if I had willed it, boom—the phone rang. It was my agent in Canada.

After some preliminaries about how I was feeling, she said, "All right, Jay, if you're feeling up to it I've got an offer for you. CTV is shooting a movie here on Baffin Island. Let me send you the script."

I was particularly intrigued because I'd always wanted to go to Baffin Island, the island next to Greenland. The setting alone made it a very interesting project for me. I told my agent, "Sure, if we can make a deal with these guys, I'll do it."

The film was based on a true story about an Inuit boy who had killed his entire family in his sleep, and the lawyer who determined that he had actually been asleep the entire time and got him off. It was a huge, highly controversial case in Canada and I was to play the attorney who represented the boy. It was fascinating to shoot where these grisly events and the trial had really played out, in a tiny town with a population of 11,000.

In May, I headed to Halifax to begin the shoot. I felt very at home in Halifax, where I'd worked before on *Love and Death on Long Island*, and I knew many of the crew members. It was about as nurturing and familiar an environment as I could ask for, which was another reason I had taken the project. My costar, a very talented actress named Kristin Booth, and I became good friends. After a week or two in Halifax, we all headed to Baffin Island for several days. Or maybe it was a week? Or ten days?

Unfortunately, there were a lot of things about shooting that movie, *Sleep Murder*, that I simply cannot remember. I didn't have any real problems at work—in remembering dialogue, or needing to halt production so I could rest, or anything like that. I got through the shoot without incident, but I had clearly gone back to work too soon. Acting was still a bit too much for my brain to handle. My circuits were overloaded. I truly needed a break.

Fortunately, the movie turned out fine. I looked okay, and my performance was certainly acceptable. At the time I thought I was doing just great, but it was only later, looking back, that I realized I had pushed myself much too hard. I got way ahead of myself in terms of recovery. To this day, I can only remember small flashes of working on that film, and that's not like me.

I came home and took the rest of the summer off, which was a very good idea. I needed the time off. I continued to gain strength and concentration and didn't even consider any more work for the moment. Then as fall approached, I got a call from ABC Family with a project that was too good to resist.

Victoria
V8W 1B2

I *Want to Marry Ryan Banks* was an ABC-TV movie, and I was offered the role of the titular character, Ryan Banks. I thought it was a fun project, especially for me, because it was about an actor who couldn't get any movies made because he had fallen off the A-list. I felt uniquely qualified to play this role. It was a wink to my real life—a good way to utilize my career baggage to my advantage.

My costar, who played my best friend and agent, was an actor I'd never met named Bradley Cooper. In the movie, his great idea was to get me a reality show à la *The Bachelor,* so everyone in America would see what a great guy I was, instead of a womanizing rat, and I would immediately catapult back to the top. Hilarity and misunderstandings with the girls ensued, with a true love happy ending. That was the movie, which was pretty forgettable. What made the experience unforgettable was to meet somebody I connected with on so many levels. Coop and I got on like a house on fire.

We had a great time shooting in Victoria for a month. Coop's girlfriend and Naomi both flew into Victoria for the long Thanksgiving weekend. Our director put on a full dinner at the Empress Hotel for the Americans who, of course, insisted on their traditional turkey. Then the four of us retreated to my resort hotel in Ucluelet on the west coast. We wrapped the movie in December and returned home to L.A. for the Christmas and New Year's holidays.

Unbeknownst to either of us, we would soon both be back in Vancouver on two separate projects. Coop got on a crime drama called *Touching Evil,* starring Jeffrey Donovan, who would go on to do *Burn Notice,* and Vera Farmiga (later to star in *Bates Motel*). Meanwhile, I got put in a series called *Tru Calling* with Eliza Dushku and Zach Galifianakis.

Tru Calling was a supernatural drama starring Eliza as a young woman who worked in a morgue; Zach played her friend and supervisor. The bodies spoke to her, asking for help, and she was able to relive their last days, trying to alter events to save their lives. I was brought on halfway through the first season to play Jack Harper, who was a foil to Eliza's character, Tru. Before, there had been a little piece missing in the show. Tru needed a combatant to go up against week in and week out. The character of Jack was a terrific addition. I certainly thought so, anyway.

Eliza and I were doing a lot of very interesting interacting. There was a great deal of conflict between us early on, then the story lines began to follow both of us as she tried to keep people alive and I tried to keep people dead. It was an interesting dynamic. The ratings numbers each week were going steadily up and up and up. Meanwhile, I was having a fantastic time with Zach and Coop on our off hours. Like me, Coop was a very adventurous eater, his particular favorite being Japanese food. Vancouver is famous for its Japanese food, so the two of us hunted down all the very best places and had plenty of superb meals together.

One night we were sitting around in my hotel room, and we just looked at each other and said at the same time, "We've got to get out of here." Neither of us could stand to stay one more night in the super-bland, corporate boring hotel where we'd been living for months on end. We found a small boutique hotel in Yale Town and checked into it the next day. This new hotel had a happening lounge and bar scene, and the crowd who hung out in that area was young and fun.

It was the right move. The little French bistro in our hotel stayed open late, and Coop and I spent a few late nights there talking about life and love and all the big questions. I had decided to propose to

Naomi, whom he had gotten to know quite well, and he listened as I psyched myself up to do the deed. I was planning a very elaborate proposal—my idea was to do it in London, where we met.

"Listen," Coop counseled. "Do it as soon as you get there. I mean, the absolute soonest you possibly can."

"Why?"

"Your nerves will be shot enough. That ring will be burning a hole in your pocket on the plane for the entire ride over . . . you don't need to be wandering around England for a week trying to maneuver her to the right place. Trust me. Get there, get to the right place, take the knee, and ask her. Do it right away."

I filed this advice away for future reference.

Sometimes we hung out with Jeffrey and Vera—just a bunch of actors sitting around bullshitting. At one point, Coop flew down to L.A. to audition for *The Wedding Crashers*. When he told me he got the part, I was thrilled for him. We both knew it was going to be a huge movie.

Coop and I spent a couple of nights a week following Zach around to the local comedy clubs he played in Vancouver. He played such tiny little venues—just Zach and his piano and a small audience who, half the time, had no idea what they were watching. People didn't know whether to laugh, be offended, or walk out . . . his shows were something else. Zach Galifianakis was absolutely brilliant, a truly singular talent, a little like the late great Andy Kaufman. Like Andy, he had moments of true comedic genius.

Zach's favorite thing to do at his performances was try to fail, miserably. Making people laugh was no challenge for him so he used to raise the bar on himself by actually trying to be unfunny. The great thing, of course, was that when he tried to not be funny, he was at his absolute most hysterical. Try as hard as he might to bomb, he never did. Coop and I watched in awe as he pulled off some amazing onstage feats.

Because I was back in my hometown, I was constantly recognized. And Zach and Coop were total unknowns. They walked around everywhere with no problem. They had no "fans" to speak of. Man, how things have changed in a few short years. . . .

We wrapped that first season of *Tru Calling,* and then I was asked to go the Monte Carlo Television Festival to help the producers sell the show internationally to the European television markets. Naomi and I headed to the TV Fest at the beginning of June and wrapped things up in a hurry. We had a wedding to attend.

Spelling Manor
Holmby Hills
90077

Tori Spelling had invited us to her wedding, but that meant we had to leave the Monte Carlo Television Festival a bit early. I very much wanted to attend the ceremony, especially to see Aaron. I wanted Naomi to meet him as he had been such a key influence in my life. Although he was no longer as big a part of my life, we were still in touch and I was anxious to introduce the two of them.

The timing was tricky; we drove to Nice, flew from Nice to Paris, then took the long flight from Paris back to L.A. A car picked us up at the airport and drove us home. The driver waited while we raced inside, showered, changed, and jumped back in the car in less than half an hour. We pulled up just in time for the sunset wedding.

There was no question that the wedding would be held at home. Just a little backyard wedding. Ha! This was a full-on Aaron Spelling production at his beloved Manor. There was no bigger or better venue in all Los Angeles, and his only daughter's wedding was everything one would expect. The ceremony was held in the motor court at the front of the property near the fountain, and it was lovely. Then all the guests walked through the Manor to attend the reception in the back.

I had been to the Manor many times to visit Aaron and had, over the years, become immune to its size and magnificence. I had forgotten how completely overwhelming this place really was the first time one saw it. Naomi walked beside me with her mouth literally falling open—frequently. She was truly in shock; she could not believe what kind of place she was walking through. Just the art alone was amazing—Monets and Chagalls everywhere you looked. There were forty-foot ceilings and magnificent room after room after room; it really was too much to take in. The sheer over-the-top opulence of the Manor was, in a word, staggering.

We finally exited the house to arrive at a huge tent in the back. There had to be at least a thousand guests mingling on the perfect grounds, with plenty of room to spare. The *90210* cast was all seated at one table, with the most elaborate place settings, decorations, and flower centerpieces I had ever seen in my life. As we took our seats, I leaned over to Naomi. "Honey," I told her, "I want you to take a really good look around. This is probably the only million-dollar wedding we will ever attend."

It was great to see everybody again. It was very much another warm reunion, though Luke was unable to attend. We all liked the groom, Charlie, a great deal. He was a writer who seemed to be a perfect match for Tori. Over the years on the show, Tori had been quite young, and not surprisingly had run through some questionable boyfriends. She had found a really good guy, and everyone at our table was happy she was settling down with him. We were happy for them both.

Aaron was visibly older and becoming more fragile every year by this time. He was also overwhelmed by well-wishers as the father of the bride. Still, he graciously took the time to sit with Naomi and me for fifteen minutes and catch up and extract a promise that I would come in to see him at his office. He was as wonderful as always, and Naomi was thrilled to finally meet the man who meant so much to me.

The whole event was so over-the-top magnificent that it would be hard for me to describe it. There's no need, anyway, as it was certainly covered extensively in magazine stories that ran for pages. I mean, Michael Bublé was the entertainment! Naomi and I were on the dance floor when the guy next to us stopped dancing and called, "Hey, Jason!" I looked over at him. It was Adam Biesk from *Teen Angel*, of all people—turned out he was a close friend of Charlie's. I was shocked to see somebody from those days. But I shouldn't have been; there were all kinds of people at that wedding. A Who's Who of Hollywood turned out for the wedding of the year.

Shaftesbury Avenue
London
W1D 3AY

The decision was made. I was going to propose to Naomi. I decided to take her back to the street corner where we met to propose, which meant I had to get her back to London under false pretenses. She was very caught up in a makeup job at the time and not in any big hurry to take a trip out of the country, or anywhere at all.

"Your brother and the new baby, we really should go see them," I told her.

"Yes, absolutely, we will . . . soon." She was not convinced.

"Luke's doing a play there . . . a limited run . . . let's go see him while we're there. We'll need to go this month. Come on, a quick trip, it'll be fun." She finally acquiesced and I picked up her diamond ring, where, as Coop had predicted, it burned a hole in my pocket the whole eleven-hour flight to London.

I did it up big. I got us a suite at the Savoy, arguably London's most famous and historic hotel, and we went to the Ivy for dinner the first night we arrived. We took a romantic little stroll after our meal and lo and behold . . . just happened to find ourselves on the street corner where we'd met. I asked Naomi to marry me, she accepted, and we immediately got into an argument about which street corner it had actually been. The reality is that we'd met on the corner of Charing

Cross Road and Shaftesbury Avenue, right in front of a Pizza Hut, which is not the slightest bit romantic.

Directly across the street is the magnificent red brick Palace Theatre, where *Les Miz* had its endless run and is still playing for all I know. "Honey, it was right there, in front of the *Les Miz* theater," she pointed.

"No, honey," I said patiently. "That would be nice, but, unfortunately, we actually met here, in front of Pizza Hut."

"Really, Jason, it was over there. I'm quite sure." The full British accent.

"And I am equally sure it was right here. Trust me, I do remember." Hey, I didn't blame the girl for wanting a more picturesque location, but we met in front of Pizza Hut.

The next night we attended the theater. Luke was starring in *When Harry Met Sally* opposite Alyson Hannigan at the Haymarket. He was great, and the audience loved him. After the show we went backstage to share the good news. Luke was, in fact, one of the first to hear it and see the ring, as this was less than twenty-four hours after I slid it onto Naomi's finger.

"It's no trip around the world, but I think we could take quite a journey together," Brandon had said to Kelly when he proposed on the show. Kelly turned Brandon and rival Dylan both down . . . in real life, I had taken Naomi around the world and she said yes. And in real life my good friend Luke could not have been happier for us both.

Atlantis Resort
Nassau
NAC: 8JNN2 M5CL8

At the beginning of the second season of *Tru Calling,* I was in New York yet again for the upfronts. I spent two days with all the FOX talent, including Mischa Barton, who was currently the hottest thing going on the show *The OC.* Naomi was working as a makeup artist on a kids' show in the Bahamas at the time, and they asked if I would appear as a guest. I grabbed the chance to see her and have a quick few days' vacation as well. Coincidentally, several of the actors from the upfronts were also scheduled to be interviewed on the same show, so we all left the hotel at around the same time and headed for La Guardia.

The first-class section of the plane to Nassau was half empty; there was just me, Mischa Barton, her mother, and a random businessman. Since we had just spent the past two days at the same event, I walked over to Mischa's aisle, where she was sitting next to her mother, hiding behind a magazine, and said hello. She lowered the magazine an inch or so as I put out my hand. "Hi, Mischa, I'm Jason Priestley, and we're going to the same event in the Bahamas together."

Her eyebrows raised a fraction. "Mmm-hmm," she said dismissively and brought the magazine back up to cover her face.

Okay, then, so it was going to be like that. I found my seat and did some work, read some scripts, whatever. We soon landed in the Bahamas, waited a bit for our bags, and then lugged them outside the airport into the hot tropical afternoon. Mischa and her mother looked around, disconcerted and lost. No one appeared to be racing to assist them.

Having stayed at the Atlantis Resort before, I knew the drill. The official Atlantis car pulled up right in front of me and the driver jumped out. "Mr. Priestley, great to see you again! How are you!" He came over, shook my hand, and took my bags.

As my old friend Cheryl Teetzel was producing the show, I figured I better help these two. I walked over to Mischa and her mom and said, "Here's the car to take us to the hotel, where we're all staying." Both women looked at me like I was the biggest asshole in the world. The driver approached, asking, "May I help?," and I said, "Yes, this is Mischa Barton; she will be staying at the hotel."

"Yes, of course. I am here to pick you up as well," the driver said and collected their luggage.

The three of us got seated in the back of the limo; I was sitting directly across from Mischa and her mother as the car prepared to leave. Mischa looked at her mother and said, "Do we have to share a car with *him*?"

"*He* can hear you, you know!" I said. "*He's* sitting right here!"

She let out an annoyed sigh and rolled her eyes, then looked out the window. We had a very silent thirty-minute ride to the resort.

WE STARTED THE second season of *Tru Calling* and got twelve weeks into it. Suddenly, a FOX executive showed up on the set to observe, then John, our show runner, called a meeting. We all sat down in the meeting and he said, "Okay, here's the deal. We're going to shoot this next episode, then FOX is canceling the show." I was absolutely staggered by the news. I had truly thought we were just beginning to hit our stride, and our ratings numbers reflected that as they continued to climb.

The season one hump was over, and we were moving right along . . . we'd brought some new and interesting characters on board: Lizzy Caplan was now on the show in a recurring role; Eric Olsen, too. I would have bet anything we would have all been there for quite some time doing that show. In this particular case, there had been a shakeup in the FOX executive ranks. The new president didn't like *Tru Calling*, especially as it was one of the old president's picks. He pretty much cleaned house. It was a purely political decision as far as I could tell, and it was quite a bummer.

We had to show up and shoot one more episode after this news . . . which was not fun for a bunch of demoralized actors. Why not just pull the plug and send us all home? Why do one more show? We all needed to be looking for a new job, for one thing, and the sooner the better. We shot the last episode, a Christmas episode called "The Lost Christmas," and that was that. I'd heard many a story like this from my buddies on other shows, of course, but it had never happened to me. That's Hollywood.

Zach and I returned to L.A., and eventually Coop's show ended, and we all returned to our lives. Mine didn't change too much, but theirs certainly did! Zach and Coop—just two guys I'd been running around with all year, carrying on, doing crazy, silly stuff all over Vancouver—would, over the next decade, star in some of the most successful motion picture comedies of all time. Man, I love Hollywood.

Warner Bros. Set
Burbank
91505

I was no longer a kid, and I was no longer living under a glaring spotlight . . . and I was glad on both counts. There had been no way to prepare for living my twenties as a suddenly famous "heartthrob." No one can give you any advice; at least I never found anyone who told me anything useful. It's an experience that's difficult to understand unless you've been through it, which is one reason why Luke, Ian, and Brian are still good friends of mine to this day. We shared a crazy experience, one that from the outside looked awesome. Fame brings so much attention and special treatment, but it's not even about you—the *real* you; it's about the character you play on television—and you know it, which makes it all pretty hollow.

I've spent most of my life being famous, and, yes, of course, much of it is fantastic. What's hard for people outside the business to understand is how overwhelming it is when fame hits a fever pitch and completely hampers your ability just to live a halfway-normal life.

When you're *too* famous, you can't go out shopping or eat dinner in a restaurant or even a bar without being interrupted by people wanting to talk—for just a minute—and get a picture or autograph or a hug.

As a twentysomething guy . . . I didn't always handle those situations all that well. I feel for anyone young undergoing that kind of sudden stardom, especially in this day where everyone has a camera and Twitter account to blast out every detail of every encounter with someone who may just be having a bad day.

My old friend Jennie had landed a starring role on the WB sitcom *That's What I Like About You*, and when she asked me to guest star a couple of times, I was happy to do so. Jennie played Valerie, a strait-laced woman living on the Upper West Side with a great job and boyfriend. Her life is turned upside down when her younger sister, Holly, played by Amanda Bynes, comes to live with her. Amanda was a very talented young actress who was being nominated for all sorts of Teen Choice awards. Both times I was on the show, I didn't even meet Amanda. She had a small group of friends, other teenagers, literally surrounding her at all times when she wasn't actually filming. They kept her in a bubble and away from everybody else.

I knew from experience how careful an actor has to be. When you're that young and making lots of money, there will always be people around who want to take advantage of you—or at least your social status and invitations. It makes it hard to have regular relation-ships when you're questioning the motives of everyone who wants to hang out with you. That, along with being relentlessly approached by fans every time you leave the house, can lead to hiding away and isola-tion, and I think *that* more than anything else is what gets to people.

It took me quite a while to learn to take fame and enjoy it for what it is, but it's hard to find that balance. This is tough especially when you're young, because famous or not, you're not particularly balanced! Fame is so fleeting . . . and to have emerged from my twenties and found a perfect level of recognition at this point in my life without falling apart is shocking. For a while there I didn't think that would be the case, and when I see somebody else struggling I have only one thought: *There but for the grace of God go I.*

One&Only Ocean Club
New Providence Island
NAC: 8JPLG M5DDY

Our wedding was simply spectacular. At the One&Only Ocean Club, a former private estate on the waterfront in the Bahamas, we hosted 145 guests. We had sent about 160 invitations, hoping that as many as could would make it to such a faraway destination. I estimate that 90 percent of our invitees showed up, which made us both so happy. The guests stayed for an entire week, with the wedding day right in the middle. It was definitely a destination wedding, an entire week of parties and entertainment and events. So many people traveled such long distances—from California and Europe, particularly—that they made a vacation of it.

Almost every single person in my family made it—my mother and stepfather, my father, my stepsisters, and of course my sister, Justine. Same with Naomi's family—almost everyone from her side came as well and looked stunning. They wore beautiful suits and hats to the wedding, in the proper English manner. Everyone who was important to us both attended; Ian was there, Jennie, Tiffani, Tori, Coop was there . . . unfortunately, Luke had a last-minute emergency, and Brian had to work. Still, most everybody I wanted to see was there.

About half the guests stayed at the Atlantis, while the other half stayed next door at the One&Only Ocean Club. Several couples brought kids, who could go to their own Kids Club. Between the two resorts there was almost too much for everyone to do. Gambling, clubbing, water parks, swimming, snorkeling, five-star restaurants, Jet Skis, sailing, barbecues on the beach, golf . . . every activity you can imagine in a wonderful paradise. The time literally flew by. The location was perfect.

The wedding ceremony itself was held late in the afternoon, after the strongest heat of the day had passed, in the gorgeous formal gardens. The reception was held afterward around the pool. A very unspoiled bride, Naomi spent the hours before the wedding doing the bridesmaids' makeup. She got so involved that she ran out of time to do her own the way she wanted, but of course she looked exquisite nevertheless. She wore a designer dress with our initials, J and N, embroidered in white on the train. No one could even see them; it was a tiny little secret hidden in the dress. She looked like an angel.

The Royal Bahamian Choir sang, and the official island Police Band played. Naomi had a great idea—as the ceremony ended and we walked back up the aisle as husband and wife, the choir burst into the classic "Oh Happy Day." It was beautiful, perfect. Being big foodies, Naomi and I both were quite picky about the reception menu, and it more than exceeded our expectations. A huge pile of stone crab claws, literally four feet high, dominated a buffet table. Lobsters, shrimp, and every kind of seafood pulled directly out the nearby Caribbean waters were exquisite. The amount of food was overwhelming and every bite of it delicious.

Naturally, we flew in our wines from California. Our friends at Behrens & Hitchcock from the Behrens family boutique winery on Spring Mountain in Napa were kind enough to custom bottle our wine. They rebottled their outstanding 2003 cabernet into double-magnum-sized bottles labeled with our wedding invitation, which was a wonderful treat. We set one out at every table, along with Veuve Clicquot and Moët White Star champagne . . . lots of it! There were loving toasts and funny toasts, and Barenaked Ladies shocked me by singing "Close to You" accompanied only by mandolins. A very cool moment for me.

A fireworks display, my surprise gift to Naomi, was a big hit. My new wife was truly surprised and moved; her reaction made me really glad that I had arranged the show. Everyone was wowed. It made for a fantastic climax to the night. Then, as if that wasn't enough, a few days later we headed off to the One&Only Palmilla in Mexico for a weeklong honeymoon with just the two of us. Hey, you only get married once . . . I figured we should do it up right!

A month later, we were at home, just an old married couple watching some silly reality show where the couple was getting married. The ceremony was at the One&Only Ocean Club, and as the bride and groom turned to walk back down the aisle, the Royal Bahamian Choir burst into "Oh Happy Day." We couldn't believe it! Copied already!

Battery Park City
New York
10280

I've been coming to Los Angeles for pilot season since the 1980s, more than twenty-five years ago. It's like spring training for actors—you'd better get your game on. It's hard work—constant memorization and then throwing it away and immediately moving on to the next thing. Pilots are shot in March or April. Actors find out if the show gets picked up in May. The show goes into production in July (for dramas) or August (for sitcoms).

Some years you get a pilot right out of the gate; other years you don't get one until the end of March. Sometimes you get nothing. That's the life of an actor, though the older I get, the more I understand the gravity of pilot season and how important it is. I've had exceptional luck with pilots; every single one that I've shot has been picked up as a show . . . and *90210* ran for ten years. I only made one pilot that didn't get picked up. It was a show for FX called *DOPE*, about drug trafficking, and it starred Keith David and me. Naturally, out of all the projects I've done, I was most surprised that that one didn't make it.

In 2005, I shot a pilot for a show called *Love Monkey* for CBS. It was picked up and turned into a midseason show being filmed in New York. Six months into our marriage Naomi and I packed up our two dogs—my beloved elderly French bulldog, Swifty, and our Alaskan Malamute, Pris—and drove all the way across country to Manhattan on the southern route, stopping in Albuquerque, Oklahoma City, and Indianapolis along the way and squeezing in a few visits to friends. It was a four-day road trip, nothing to it.

We arrived in New York and had to find a place to live. Naomi found an apartment in Battery Park City that we both loved—actually not far at all from our old loft, the scene of many a good time. *Love Monkey* was a show about the music industry, starring Tom Cavanagh as a guy who started his own indie record label with a bunch of friends who helped him through his trials and tribulations at work and in his personal life. Judy Greer, Larenz Tate, Chris Wiehl, Katherine LaNasa, and I rounded out the regular cast. As much as I liked working on the show, and all my fellow cast mates, I would have liked to have had a bigger role, mainly because I like to work and have never been one to sit around, but at least I had a good time hanging out again in our old stomping grounds during my free time.

We started shooting in October and shot eight episodes . . . then the network execs canceled the show. Only three episodes ever aired. Too bad . . . it was a fun show, and I thought everybody involved did a great job. I thought that maybe the early shows focused a bit too much on the character's job in the music industry as opposed to his relationships, and audiences had a hard time becoming invested, but who knows? Believe me, you never really know. But after just a few episodes, when ratings did not deliver, the network pulled the plug. They don't mess around these days.

Fortunately, my wife was much more productive. Naomi was doing some very cool stuff. She had a great time in New York that winter, nailing down all kinds of amazing gigs. New York is the center of the fashion world, and Naomi became an in-demand makeup artist that year—for magazine cover shoots and editorials, but the coup de grâce was the Victoria Secret Fashion Show. That winter in New York was worth it just for that.

After our work in New York, we repacked the car and drove back across country, the northern route this time, visiting Chicago and Mount Rushmore along the way. We also made a quick stop in Sun Valley to visit some friends and ski, and somehow we stayed for two entire weeks. My agents were calling me nonstop, telling me to get home for the rest of pilot season, but the snow was so unbelievable that we kept deciding to stay for just one more day.

We did eventually return home, and not surprisingly I didn't get a pilot that year.

The Beverly Hilton Hotel
Beverly Hills
90210

Even if I'd wanted to, I could never really leave *Beverly Hills 90210* behind. It was a cultural phenomenon that continued to live on and on. In 2006, the entire original cast made an appearance at the official "Season One Boxed Set DVD" release party at the Beverly Hilton Hotel in Beverly Hills. It was a great chance to catch up with everyone—a couple of people had new partners and Tori, naturally, was accompanied by her new significant other.

When Tori left Charlie, after only a couple of years, for a married Canadian actor named Dean McDermott, it made a big splash in the entertainment news. I was shooting *Love Monkey* at the time in New York, and my costar mentioned something about it to me.

"Hey, man, your old buddy Tori hooked up with my old buddy Dean. You're really going to like him, he's a great guy," Tom had told me.

"Good, glad to hear it," I said, though I was sorry to hear about Tori's split. I liked Charlie. Still, fine, it was her life, I wanted Tori to be happy, and I trusted Tom's judgment. At the event, we were all being pulled in every direction, alone and in various combinations, by the media and the paparazzi most of the evening. Finally, while taking a breather, at some point I found myself inside the Hilton, in a hallway, with Dean standing alone nearby.

I walked over to him, extended my hand, and said, "Hi, Dean, Jason Priestley. Welcome to our big dysfunctional family."

He stared down at my hand, then back up at my face. No handshake, no response, nothing. I was somewhat taken aback by this reaction.

"Well. Tom Cavanagh speaks highly of you," I said.

"Oh yeah?" Dean said aggressively.

"Yeah. For some reason, he seems to think you're a nice guy." I turned and left. Haven't spoken to him since.

I had a much more pleasant introduction to Brian Austin Green's new girlfriend. He was dating a young actress he'd met guest-starring on Kelly Ripa's sitcom *Hope & Faith*. Megan Fox was sweet and almost painfully shy. She was a natural beauty with a fresh-faced look—not surprising as she was only in her early twenties. She stood quietly off to the side as Brian was interviewed on the red carpet, fidgeting a bit and playing with her long hair as she waited patiently. None of the paparazzi gave her a second look.

A year later she would be one of the hottest female movie stars in the world. Once again, you gotta love Hollywood.

About a month after the DVD event, I happened to be home watching the local news one night, something I rarely got to do. Tori Spelling's yard sale made the broadcast that night. Apparently, she and Dean were moving now that she was pregnant. Her personal style had changed. She was getting rid of everything. That's what she told the press. Suddenly, I saw my very own wedding invitation on-screen. Apparently, it had gone for five bucks, including a personal autograph by Tori. She sold my wedding invitation to a stranger *for five dollars.*

I turned and looked at my wife, and she at me. We were both stunned. I couldn't believe how violated I felt. I couldn't understand how Tori didn't find that kind of behavior inappropriate. Sure, she got rid of everything she could, apparently, including plenty of personal mementos from her own fairly recent wedding, but that was her own stuff. Her privacy was one thing; mine was another. I couldn't wrap my mind around how she thought this was okay to do to a friend and coworker of nearly a decade. Naomi and I were both gobsmacked, to use a good English word.

I was already far from enchanted with Tori's new husband. This was just icing on the cake.

The producers of Tori and Dean's ubiquitous reality show do make a point of asking me to appear on every single iteration. So far I haven't been able to find the time.

"Pleasantville" USA

A t the beginning of Naomi's pregnancy that came along in our second year of marriage, we had all these wonderful ideas that we'd be able to live in our 1928 house on a hill with fifty-two steps to the front door once we had kids. We figured, hey, we'll throw up some gates and the kid will be fine. We had no idea of the realities of strollers and diaper bags and all the stuff a baby would need.

Naomi was about six months along when I was sitting in the living room, watching the NHL playoffs on TV one day. All of a sudden, the front door swung open and my pregnant wife stood there holding five bags of groceries. Sweat had broken out on her forehead. She did not look pleased. "We're moving!" she said.

"Sure, baby, whatever you want to do. You want to move, let's move. Good idea!" I told her.

She was in serious nesting mode, all right. During that last trip up all those stairs, carrying bags of groceries—something in her just snapped. She got serious about finding the right place to live. Within a week, she called asking me to meet her to look at the perfect place she had found for us in the Valley. As I got closer and closer to the address, I realized that I was just a few blocks from where Frank Levy had lived when I first arrived in Los Angeles, in his picture-perfect neighborhood. Frank, sadly, had passed on in the 1990s. He was a good guy;

it was a sad day for me when he died. After we parted ways, I did not
have a manager again for ten years.

This neighborhood was still truly something special, the ideal
small-town USA look and feel, hidden away behind the crossroads
of some of the busiest freeways in L.A. In addition to looking like a
movie set, it was a friendly and tight-knit community with lots of kids
around. We put an offer in that day and bought it that night. Naomi
was in no mood to fool around.

Next we were on to the great name search, which lasted for months.
We had all the books full of baby names. We both loved the name
Ava but kept discarding it because at the time there was a run on that
name. Everywhere we turned, someone else was naming their daughter Ava. One night, a friend of ours was listening to our discussion and
said, "Who cares what everyone else is doing? You love the name Ava,
she'll be *your* Ava, call her what you want." It was very good advice.

On the night our daughter was born in 2007, I spent the night in
the hospital with both her and my wife. Seeing Ava's birth was a life-
altering experience for me. Until that moment, our daughter had been
very theoretical to me. Of course I watched Naomi's stomach expand
and felt our daughter moving around inside, but the baby just wasn't
real to me. The moment I saw baby Ava, everything changed for me in
a profound and serious way. The gravity of the situation struck me: this
tiny little being was completely dependent on her mother and me for
her existence and survival. The weight of that responsibility struck me
immediately, and all my loving and protective instincts kicked into high
gear. Or to put it more simply: one look at her face and I was a goner.

Of course, we got very little sleep that night. I awoke early the next
morning, said good-bye to my girls, and drove back to the Warner
Ranch, where I was shooting my new television series *Side Order of
Life*. I was completely scattered and emotional and for once in my life
not well prepared. I had to do a long driving scene where I was in the
car talking to someone on the phone. I pasted the dialogue pages all
over the inside of the car so I could be "driving" and look casually
down and remember what the hell I was supposed to say next.

My world had shifted on its axis; I would never be the same again.

Cedars-Sinai
West Hollywood
90048

Naomi spent a couple of days in the hospital recovering, and then I wheeled my wife out to the waiting car. We carefully put Ava in her brand-new car seat for the very first time and I drove home. The three of us! Naomi and I kept looking at each other in shock, like we'd just gotten away with something.

Of course, outside the hospital, a group of photographers lay in wait, trying to get the first shot of Ava. We did a lot of maneuvering to sneak out of the place without a tabloid photographer chasing us down for the first newborn shot. My agent at the time recommended that we make a deal for an official photo shoot so that we could control the situation, not a tabloid person. It's an unfortunate reality of the world today that when anybody famous has a baby, it brings out aggressive tabloid photographers, trying to be first, looking for that money shot. Believe me, to them it's all about money. The main reason celebrities set up official "baby shoots" is to take any profit for aggressive photographers out of the equation. Nobody needs to be surrounded by flashbulbs as they try to take a days-old baby home for the very first time.

It was strange and wonderful and exciting to unload our tiny little infant and take her inside with us, but we were pretty sure we had it knocked. We'd both read plenty of parenting and baby books, not to mention we'd spent a great deal of time around friends with children. We were a bit overconfident, actually, because we knew nothing about having a newborn. Nothing. I got Naomi settled in bed, Ava resting in a bassinet next to her. Right from the start, Ava had an excellent appetite and breast-fed with no problems. Everything was fine, until she started crying—which she proceeded to do for the next twenty hours straight, no breaks. We had a colicky newborn on our hands.

As first-time parents, we were completely dumbfounded. We tried everything. Feeding her. Changing her. Picking her up. Burping her. Walking around with her. Putting her in her bassinet. Swaddling her. Nothing worked, and Naomi and I just looked at each other as the hours wore on, becoming more and more frantic. This baby had been an absolute angel in the hospital, with barely a peep out of her the first couple days of her life. Now this tiny little creature would not stop screeching at an earsplitting level. It was shockingly loud.

I finally found a way to carry Ava around, walking with a very slight bounce that seemed to soothe her; also, she had worn herself out. After her epic crying bout, she finally fell asleep the next morning, a full twenty hours after I had so happily put her and her mom to bed. Naomi and I were completely hollow-eyed, worn-out, and shell-shocked, and quite a bit less sure about our parenting knowledge than we'd been just a day or so before.

We quickly learned that the problem was Naomi's diet; she had to stick to very simple food while breast-feeding. Anything with the slightest amount of nuts or soy or dairy caused an immediate and dreadfully negative reaction in Ava. So Naomi lived on plain chicken, rice, and arugula for the next nine months. In less than two weeks, she was back to her prepregnancy weight—the strict diet plus breast-feeding caused any baby weight to disappear in a flash.

My job was head cook. I made sure that plenty of the extremely limited foods the girls could tolerate were stocked and ready to make at all times. Naomi and I went into full swing with our baby-raising diet, and our team effort really paid off. Ava was happy and healthy. Meanwhile, Naomi's mum and London friends sent real, truly English

Cadbury chocolate for when she could eat it again and she got her stockpile ready. She'd given up everything else without a murmur, but when it came time, she wanted some chocolate, stat!

We were the absolutely classic new parents, completely spellbound by our baby. We spent hours just watching Ava, waiting to see what she would do next. We could not get enough of her. We snapped photos, shot videos, and took her everywhere—you name it, we did it. It was no surprise that my old friend Jann Wenner made a great offer for Ava's official baby pictures. He sent a first-class photographer over to our house, who took a stunning family photo of the three of us in the backyard. Then he put it on the cover of *US* magazine. Baby Ava was already a cover girl!

Rainbow Bridge

Swifty held on for a week after Ava was born. He was old and sick with cancer, and an untreatable tumor was pressing against his lungs. There was nothing more the vet could do for him. They had told me I would know when the time came to put him down. Until then, as long as he was eating, I should just keep him comfortable and happy. I was grateful to have the warning so I had time to accustom myself to the idea of life without him.

Ava was less than a week old the day Swifty refused to eat. As we approached the twenty-four-hour mark with no food, I knew the time had come. I called the vet and carried Swifty out to the car with me for the very last time. As I pulled out and headed for the vet's office, Swifty stood up and looked directly at me. He was giving me a very fixed stare, as though he was trying to hold me in his memory. His breathing became very loud and labored. I knew he was dying.

I pulled over only a couple of blocks from my house, took him out of the car, sat on the grass, and gave him a big hug. I was holding him when I felt the very last beat of his heart against mine and saw the light go out in his eyes. My Swifty, who had been with me for fourteen years. That dog had seen some things in his life! He had more frequent flyer miles that most people I know.

That was really, really hard. In the midst of my elation about the birth of my first child, I lost one of my oldest and dearest friends. Swifty was such a good boy. I knew in my heart that he had held on until Ava arrived.

Warner Ranch
Burbank
91522

I worked frequently as a director because I very much enjoyed taking material on the printed page and taking it all the way through to a finished product on-screen. That was my challenge as a director. Actors have to be very self-involved: worried about their timing, hitting their marks, their motivation, how they look, you name it. Looking at the big picture as director was a very different and rewarding challenge. Many, many actors think they want to be a director until they give it shot, and then they quickly decide it's too much work. It's an awful lot of painstaking mundane preparation and a tremendous amount of work for very little glory, toiling in the background to make it all happen. Acting of course is just the opposite—less work, all the attention.

I'd heard rumors about a remake of *Beverly Hills 90210* for a couple of years, and in 2008 it eventually got up and running. Once production became official, an offer came in for me to reprise my role as Brandon, something I had no interest in doing. I couldn't really see how Brandon Walsh would fit into this new version. Directing, however, was another story. I got booked to direct the seventeenth episode of the first season, so I watched every episode in order to be fully up to speed and know what was going on with the story line.

The show really had little to do with the original besides the title and original premise. It was a completely different production—a very good-looking show. They certainly had all the toys and bells and whistles to make it look superluxe and impressive—not exactly what I recalled from the original! Jennie was playing Kelly again on the new show. The woman who played her mother, the actress Ann Gillespie, was also back, and she was someone I was very happy to see again after fifteen years or so. It was a quick, enjoyable job but not even close to any kind of reunion; this new show was a completely different production from what I remembered.

I HAD KNOWN producer Brenda Hampton since her first job writing an episode of *Sister Kate*. Over the intervening years she'd created the hit show *7th Heaven* and had become a powerful producer. Her latest project was a new show called *The Secret Life of the American Teenager*. I originally signed on to direct two episodes and while I was there, the show was picked up, so I signed on for three more episodes over the next six months. Obviously, the cast was a bunch of young actors finding their way, and I certainly had a bit of experience in that department. I hoped that having me around was a good experience for those guys, and I tried to help them out as much as I could.

In a great stroke of luck, the show was filmed literally ten minutes away from our new house, and my hours were extremely civilized for once. Brenda liked to wrap up work by 3:00 P.M. every day, so that couldn't have worked out better. Naomi and I were determined to do it all ourselves, with no outside help, and fortunately my schedule worked perfectly with a new baby. I worked and then came home every afternoon to take care of Naomi and Ava and do all the shopping and cooking. It was an ideal situation for the whole first year of Ava's life.

South Kensington
London
SW7 5BD

Vanessa Redgrave slapped me in the face. It was my fault, of course.
I got offered a part in a BBC miniseries, called *Day of the Triffids,* that was to shoot in London. The series was based on the famous science fiction novel by British author John Wyndham, about a postapocalyptic London terrorized by flesh-eating plants. The story had been filmed before, several times; it was a classic B movie in the 1960s, as well as an earlier BBC production in the early 1980s. This new version updated and modernized the story while staying fairly true to the original material in the book.

The cast was all-star: Dougray Scott, Joely Richardson, Eddie Izzard, Vanessa Redgrave . . . and me! We were off to England for ten weeks. Naomi and I set up house in a rented flat in South Kensington. The work went well. I had one memorable scene that called for Vanessa to try to hit me; I was supposed to catch her hand before any damage was done. I felt pretty confident about my superior reflexes. "Go on, Vanessa, try to hit me. I'll get my hand up there and stop it."

Of course there were a bunch of extras all around us, filming in close quarters, and my arm got stuck. I couldn't get my hand up in time so I got smacked. She's quick! She was quite apologetic, but it was completely my fault. I was happy to take my licks from a legend!

During production there was a freak snowstorm in London, with about eighteen inches of snow on the ground. It was absolutely beautiful, though the storm shut the city down. City officials simply did not know how to handle it and everything was basically crippled. Production went on, however, and it made the set stunningly beautiful: London, covered in snow, looking very Dickensian and classically British.

Our year-old daughter was going through a phase where she was mad about dinosaurs—she just could not get enough. We were only a couple of blocks from the Natural History Museum, so we used to take her nearly every day to their world-famous dino exhibit, which absolutely transfixed her. Ava adored London—riding the tube everywhere, visiting her beloved dinos, eating Chinese food at Mr. Chow's. She was already quite a foodie, our once-colicky little daughter now a fearless eater, never picky. It was a wonderful trip.

BECAUSE MY DAUGHTER was an American, I wanted to be absolutely certain that I could always be guaranteed to get back into America from that point on. I was also anxious to finally vote. I'd left Canada before I was of legal voting age, and in the decades I'd been in the United States, I'd had work permits and green cards and all kinds of different statuses. If I became an official citizen, I could finally have my say in the political process, which of course seemed much more pressing. I think it's true of anyone who has a child: you suddenly become much more concerned about the kind of world your child will inherit, and you get quite a bit more involved in various issues and causes.

I'd been here for so long, lived in two of America's greatest cities, and had traveled through almost every state. It was exciting to make it official. I took my test, became a citizen, and now thoroughly enjoy being part of the democratic process!

"Pleasantville" USA

O h, the things you learn once you become a member of the parenting club! One night Naomi said to me out of the blue, "Want to have a boy?"

"That would be great!" I answered.

"Okay then, now's the time!" We got busy, and her promise was borne out by the ultrasound several months later—there was our boy. Naomi was that in tune with her body. I learned that male sperm are quicker and lighter than female sperm; they reach the egg fast but are weak. Female sperm are bigger and stronger and live longer, but move more slowly. Some people believe that by conceiving on the day a woman is actually ovulating, you should have a boy. By conceiving on a day before ovulation, you should have a girl. This natural plan certainly worked for us!

Naomi was working as the makeup artist for a production company during her second pregnancy. One of their productions in 2009 was the HGTV television show *Design Star*. She was approached by a producer one day, who asked if she would consider allowing them to redo a room in our house for a special celebrity edition of the show. Each of the three show finalists would redo one room in a celebrity's home. Naomi, of course, would be perfect for a nursery.

"Sounds great," Naomi said. "Who else are you thinking of for the episode?" She knew they needed at least two other celebrities to appear on the episode.

"I don't know, you're the first person I've approached," the producer said. "Why, do you have any suggestions?"

Immediately, Naomi said, "How about Tiffani Thiessen? I know she's looking to have some work done on her house."

Naomi was excited; me, not so much. I felt a great deal of trepidation when Naomi approached me with the idea that night. Since my *90210* days I had guarded my privacy so fiercely when it came to my home; it's the one area I'd always tried to keep off limits. I felt that whatever small amount of privacy was afforded me had to be very carefully guarded. As I got older, though, I mellowed and relaxed a bit. I began to think I had made too big a deal out of it all when I was a kid. And so it came to pass that the four of us were two of the three celebrity couples featured on the "Make Over a Room in a Celebrity's Home" episode. Kathy Griffin was the third. Her staff office was redone, while Tiffani got a new guest bedroom.

Naomi, Ava, and I stayed at a hotel near the beach in Santa Monica for a few nights while they redid the room. Ava was in heaven. Ever since she was the tiniest little girl, she thought hotel life was the best thing ever. The three of us had so much fun. We drove down to the beach every day and went out for meals. Tiffani and Brady came over one night and joined up with us because they were out of their house as well for the same few days. Of course, we all speculated about what they were doing to our houses and if this had really been a good idea or not. The show gave us a nice chance to catch up.

We came home to discover that *Design Star* Dan Vickery had done a fantastic job on our nursery. It was beautiful, restful, and sophisticated, not at all babyish. We couldn't have been happier with the results—and his redo was quite convenient as our son, Dash, showed up pretty shortly afterward.

The second he arrived, I was once again weak at the knees and simply lost—he had the cutest little face. In fact, Dashiell was gorgeous! This time I was able to stay with Naomi and Dash the entire time they were in the hospital, without having to leave for work. Right from the start, he was such a good little guy, good eater, good sleeper, very little trouble. This time, we were far more on top of things. When we got Dash home and the colic started, we knew right away what needed to happen.

It was diet time for Naomi again. I have to give her credit—once again she lived uncomplainingly on chicken and arugula nonstop for months and months. Once in a while she might have a Trader Joe's egg roll, which she could get away with. Again, she stockpiled her Cadbury. I don't have much of a sweet tooth and don't eat chocolate, which is a good thing, because to have indulged while she was prohibited would have sparked a riot!

I had to head off on location for a short time, so Naomi's mother showed up to help while I was gone. It was hard for me to leave at that time. I could not, in all good conscience, have left my wife alone with a toddler and a newborn. I raced home as soon as I could to return to my disgruntled daughter and adorable son. Ava was not amused by her brother's arrival, and for the first six months or so of his life she basically pretended he wasn't there. Maybe she was hoping he would go back to where he came from. Eventually, begrudgingly, she faced the fact that he was here to stay and from that point on has been perfectly cheerful.

They are the whole world to me.

The Lot (Again)
90046

Over the course of directing a web series called *The Lake* for Warner Bros., I became friendly with the show's two writers, Meredith and Marcy. While we edited *The Lake,* they both kept talking to me about a writer named Sheri Elwood and a pilot she had written called *Meet Phil Fitz*. I had to read this script, they kept telling me. I had to meet Sheri. I was perfect to play the lead . . . and so on and so on.

Nine times out of ten, when somebody talks up a writer or piece of material to this extent it's a big disappointment. I'd heard stuff like this for years. But these women were relentless. After hearing about this pilot for weeks nonstop, I gave in and said, "Have Sheri e-mail me the pilot. Jeez, I'll read it, okay? Just send it to me." This was just another thing I had to do; I certainly wasn't excited about it.

A couple of weeks later, a script landed in my in-box. I opened it immediately because I wanted to get this over with, and then I realized that this was, hands down, the best piece of material I had read in years. Richard (Fitz) Fitzpatrick is the son of Ken Fitzpatrick, founder of the family car dealership, Fitzpatrick Motors. Fitz works alongside his father, selling cars. Just like his father, he is an alcoholic, rageaholic, sex-addicted, beyond-deluded guy who thinks he is absolutely awesome. In his mind, he's perfection; in reality he is completely morally bankrupt. Imagine the absolute polar opposite of Brandon Walsh, times ten. Naturally, this made it an even more appealing role for me.

I sent Sheri an e-mail literally titled "OMG—Best thing I've read in years." In it, I hit her with a bunch of questions. What's the deal with the show? Is it set up anywhere? How is the casting coming? How do I meet you? What do I have to do to play this guy?

Her e-mail back explained that the show was set up at HBO Canada and that she was coming to L.A. in a couple of weeks to hold auditions. She asked if I could come in and read. Of course I could! I told her that I would be wherever, whenever she wanted to see me. We sent a couple more e-mails back and forth about the character over the next two weeks as I prepared, and then it was audition time.

Amazingly enough, I met Sheri at the Lot, on Formosa and Santa Monica, where I'd gone to audition for *Beverly Hills 90210* twenty years before. I hadn't been on that lot since! It's a tiny little facility, not a huge studio lot like Paramount or FOX with their acres and acres of land and hundreds of stages and offices. Nothing ever shoots there. It's an unlikely little location, nearly hidden, and in all the auditions I'd been on since then I hadn't had one reason to go back.

This is where Aaron's office used to be, I thought as I drove onto the Lot. I took this as a good omen. The audition for *90210* had turned out well; hopefully my luck here would hold.

I heard that Sheri was being assisted by a casting director who specialized in finding Canadian talent in Los Angeles. When I walked into the office, I realized it was none other than Libby Goldstein, the casting director I had used on *Kiss Tomorrow Goodbye,* so that was one friendly relationship in my favor. I read for Sheri, running a few scenes a few different ways, and then put it all on tape. Sheri was excited at the end of our meeting and told me how much she appreciated me coming in.

"You're the one for this, Jason. I just have to send this up to the network in Toronto so the HBO execs can sign off on you."

"Great," I said, and we shook hands as I prepared to leave. She held my hand for an extra second, looked me right in the eye, and emphasized, "Really, I think you're perfect for Fitz."

I left feeling very high. The whole meeting had an eerie déjà vu feeling—from the location, of course, but right down to that happy hopeful feeling of knowing I not only had killed my audition, I also had Sheri firmly in my camp . . . just as Aaron had been on my side so many years before with Brandon.

Two days later, I got the call. I was going to play the role of Richard Fitzpatrick. Next came a bunch of chemistry readings on the Lot to find the rest of the cast . . . including the crucial role of Larry, who plays Fitz's conscience. When Ernie Grunwald came in, that was that. We hit it off immediately; we just had so much fun playing off each other. It was shaping up to be a fantastic project and I could not have been happier. I had a new son and a new role.

Wolfville
BP4 1E8

One day at a casting meeting on the Lot, Sheri idly mentioned that they were finalizing where *Fitz* would shoot. One of the possibilities was Wolfville, Nova Scotia. At that time, Nova Scotia was giving out huge tax credits to attract the film and television industry, so there was a big incentive to shoot there.

"I'm quite familiar with Wolfville," I told her.

"No way! No one's ever even heard of the place," she scoffed. "I mean that itty-bitty little town in the middle of the Annapolis Valley—"

"Yes, where they produce wine," I interrupted. "It's the heart of wine country for Nova Scotia. I have most certainly been there, looking for wines."

Sure enough, that's where we wound up shooting. It came down to the fact that there was an abandoned Kia car dealership at the end of one street. The owners had moved everything to a new dealership a mile away, and the empty place left an absolutely perfect set for Fitz. The tiny little town where the abandoned dealership lay was named New Minas. It stood in for Anytown USA, with its big box stores, fast-food restaurants, and boring main strip. Just your typical little drab small town with Walmart as the biggest retailer and the local car dealer at the end of the main drag. It was the absolute perfect location for *Call Me Fitz*.

The great thing about New Minas was that it was book-ended by two absolutely beautiful little storybook Victorian towns, Wolfville and Kentville, where all the cast and crew stayed. There was no way I could live that far away from Ava and newborn Dash, so the whole family came with me. Naomi packed up the kids and the dog and set up house.

We rented a great rural property with an absolutely huge front yard. There was no kind of fencing or anything way out in the country, but there was plenty of room for our German shepherd, Deckard, to roam the vast property alone. Every morning when we played fetch, I threw the ball as far as I could and it was always still within our yard, no matter what direction. This was real country living, quite a change for us, but we all loved it.

I came home from work one night on a very typical evening. I filled the food bowl and put it down for Deckard. I was peeling carrots with Ava, showing her how to use a peeler, when we heard a knock on the back door. That was quite unusual this far out; people didn't tend to drop by. A woman was standing on our back porch looking absolutely stricken. "Do you have a dog?" she asked.

"Yes, a German shepherd," I said, not worried. I had just seen him.

"I think we hit him," she said. I tore through the house and ran all the way up the driveway. I could see his form lying in the middle of the road. As I got closer, I watched to see if his belly was moving at all, but he was absolutely still. The woman's husband had pulled his car into our driveway and was sitting in the driver's seat with his face in his hands, completely distraught. As I leaned over Deckard's body, the woman tried to explain.

"He just came bounding out of that ditch. We could not avoid hitting him. I am so sorry. My husband is so upset he can't even bring himself to speak. We have dogs, we can't imagine how this happened, we're just so, so sorry. . . ."

"It's all right, it's all right. I know it was an accident," I told her as I leaned over the body of my dog, who fortunately appeared to have died instantly. At least he hadn't suffered. After the people left, I carried him back inside and put his body in the garage. There was nothing I could do that night. But little Ava was very curious. "Daddy, Daddy, what's wrong with Deckard?" she kept asking.

I was not anxious to introduce the concept of death to our two-year-old, plus I was still in shock at how Deckard had been there with us in the kitchen one moment and dead the next. "Honey, he's just sleeping. He's very tired and needs to rest in the garage tonight."

Naomi and I were completely freaked out, but trying to hold it together and behave normally during dinner. The whole incident was so strange. Deckard liked to stick close to home as he was very attentive and protective of the family members. He liked to stay on the lookout. After we ate, I had to go to the garage to pick something up and of course Ava followed. She leaned curiously over Deckard and looked at his body for a long time. "Deckard's dead, isn't he, Daddy?"

"Well, honey . . . yes, he is," I said, and prepared myself for a tricky conversation. As far as I knew, we had never discussed death with her, but clearly she knew a dead dog when she saw one.

"Okay," she said, and looked at him for a few more moments. "Okay, Deckard, come back inside now and play," she said, and waited expectantly. Even in the midst of my sorrow, I was fascinated by how her mind worked. Her concept of death was a bit shaky; she didn't seem to realize it was a permanent condition.

"Not now, honey. Deckard needs to stay out here in the garage."

"Okay, Daddy," she said and back we went inside the house.

I loaded Deckard into the back of the minivan the next morning on the way to work. My driver took his body to the vet and brought back his ashes. That weekend, Naomi put Dash in a baby Bjorn and we all headed out into the woods where we used to walk all the time with Deckard. We spread his ashes out there and explained the ceremony as well as we could to Ava. Our two-year-old was forcing us to deal with the big questions of life and death. It was amazing what my kids were teaching me every single day. They had become the center of my life. I could not even remember a time before them.

Grimaldi Forum Monaco
Monte Carlo
98000

Working as a comedic actor on *Call Me Fitz* has been one of the great joys of my professional career. Fitz always seems fresh to me, because it's something different and outrageous every week. Playing the antihero—the anti-Brandon, if you will—is refreshing. There are no rules, no boundaries as to how far I can push things, which is a great exercise for me. Everything I didn't get to do as Brandon—I do it all and more this time around. Keeping the stories funny, yet still believable, is the dance we do on the show. We have to root the craziness in some kind of reality. I will keep playing Fitz until somebody forces me to quit doing it.

Not only has *Fitz* been a hit on HBO Canada, it's somewhat of a cult secret in the United States, as viewers can catch it on DirecTV or online. In another pleasant departure from *90210, Fitz* has been critically acclaimed, winning all kinds of awards in Canada and at the Monte Carlo Television Festival. The festival, where I'd gone many a time over the years to promote other shows, is always an incredible production. The awards were founded fifty-seven years ago by Prince Rainier to honor outstanding television programming from all over the world, and they've been handing out Golden Nymphs ever since to winners from every country.

I was nominated for my first Golden Nymph Award, for Outstanding Actor on a Comedy TV Series, for my work on *Fitz* in 2011. Most of the cast was there, as I was, because the show itself had also been nominated. I didn't win, though I did pick up a Canadian Comedy Award for my work that year. The next year I was nominated again . . . and I won! Of course, in classic Jason Priestley style, I wasn't there to collect my award in person. I was directing an episode of the supernatural drama *Haven* during the awards, but plenty of my *Fitz* costars were present, including my friend and costar who plays my conscience, Ernie Grunwald.

I was standing on a set in Nova Scotia at a slow time, in between setups, when I felt the phone in my pocket buzz. I looked at the text from Ernie. "And the winner is . . ." he sent.

Very funny, I thought. A minute later the phone buzzed again and I pulled it back out of my pocket. "Jason Priestley!" said the text. He went up onstage to accept for me, which was absolutely perfect, of course.

Fitz and *Haven* share a crew, and our script supervisor on both shows, Joanne Hagen, happened to be standing next to me. "Hey, Joanne!" I said. "I just won a Golden Nymph at the Monte Carlo Film Festival!"

"Well, Mr. Priestley, congratulations," she said. Very dry.

Beverly Hills 90210

Look, I'm not a "reunion" kind of a guy. I'm always looking ahead to the next thing. Still, Chuck Rosin, our original show runner, made note of the *90210*'s class graduation date. An e-mail popped up in my in-box. "You do realize, it was twenty years ago this month that you all graduated from West Beverly High School . . ." it began.

To be perfectly honest, I hadn't remembered, but I did appreciate that he remembered and made the grand gesture of hosting a "high school reunion" of sorts. We were all invited to a Sunday barbecue at his home. In the middle of a record heat wave, a bunch of us gathered in his yard, twenty years later: me, Luke, Jennie, and Gabby. Mike Cudlitz, who acted on the show in the college years but was the full-time construction foreman the entire time, was also there—a great guy and definitely part of the family.

I caught up with Luke about a film he had recently directed. We all texted Brian nonstop in New York, where he was working. Ian was in Vegas doing a Chippendale's engagement, so we Skyped him in. Jennie was headed off to see his show with Shannen, immediately after the picnic—they had reconnected when they both appeared on the new version of the show and were friends again. I didn't see Tori. The triangle again, just like back in the day.

The reunion was casual and relaxed. As Naomi and I left, it dawned on me that I didn't need to "reunite" with anyone, because most of the cast and crew are still very much a part of my life. Luke and Ian have remained great friends throughout the years. The same goes for Brian, whose kid will be attending the same school as mine next year. We can attend PTA meetings together! I talk to Gabby frequently; Tiff and Brady are two of our closest friends; Jennie and I will always be friendly; and KC is my kids' godfather.

School's been out for a long, long time—*90210*ver—but the friendships and the memories will last my entire lifetime.

"Pleasantville" USA

No sharks, tornadoes, or special effects, but our little road trip film *Cas & Dylan* was a pick at the Atlantic Film Festival in Halifax, Nova Scotia, in the fall of 2013. The screening, which was held in a theater with probably six hundred seats, played right in the middle of festival week to a packed house. I introduced the film to the audience and then took my seat. I enjoyed the reactions as they laughed at all the right places, didn't laugh at any of the wrong ones, and sniffled through the end.

When the lights came up, I got one of the biggest surprises of my career: a spontaneous standing ovation. This was an experience I had never had before—sitting in the audience while everyone stood, faced me, and clapped. It was a completely different feeling than being on stage; I was literally surrounded by people cheering my film! The clapping seemed to go on for five minutes, though it was probably barely one. I was stunned—and so surprised and moved.

Directing Tatiana and Richard in *Cas & Dylan* was definitely a highlight, but as I'm sure you've noticed if you've gotten this far, I am wired to reach the highest level I can, whether that's acting, racing cars, directing . . . you name it. So, what mountain can I climb next? I have a few ideas percolating in my mind for my next project . . . something bigger and better than I've ever tried before. Stay tuned.

Meanwhile, the Priestley family is thriving in Pleasantville. Naomi has just wrapped up a cosmetics project with Brooke Burke, she has her own web show called *Shoot the Shit with Jack and Nimh*, and she recently became a certified spin instructor. Nearly fifteen years into our relationship, she is more captivating than ever before.

Dash is a happy little guy; he loves to swim, drum, and play outside, and he just started his first year of "school." And five-year-old Ava? She's obsessed with iCarly. She came to me the other day and said, "Daddy, I want to be one of those people on the web!"

What do you think . . . should I introduce her to my agent?

Epilogue

Growing up isn't easy for anyone. And growing up in the public eye is especially difficult. We've all seen the examples. And I'm sure we'll all see many, many more. When I came to Los Angeles at seventeen, I really thought that I had it all figured out and that I was an adult. Boy, was I wrong. When I started *Sister Kate* at twenty I thought I was grown up—nope. *Beverly Hills 90210* at twenty-one, still a mere child. I didn't finally get around to growing up until I was thirty years old. But in a strange way, that's Hollywood. And Hollywood's not going to change.

I feel incredibly fortunate to have always had my work that I love— to inspire, to motivate, and to save me. This industry is difficult, and audiences can be fickle. I have been incredibly blessed with a long and vibrant career that is still going strong today. A lot of that is due to hard work, and some of it is just dumb luck. But you know what they say: I'd rather be lucky than good any day!

About the Author

Jason Bradford Priestley was born in Vancouver, British Columbia. He first appeared on television in 1975, and since then has become one of the most versatile talents in the entertainment business. As a veteran both in front of and behind the camera, in *Call Me Fitz,* he not only stars in the lead role of Richard Fitzpatrick, but he also produces and directs the series. Priestley is best known for his role as Brandon Walsh on the hit FOX series *Beverly Hills 90210,* which ran from 1990 to 2000.